The MAILBOX®
The Education Center®

Leveled Skill Builders

grades 4–5

Differentiated Practice Pages Covering Skills in These Key Areas

Language Arts

- **Language Conventions**
- **Word Analysis**
- **Reading Comprehension**
- **Research and Inquiry**

Math

- **Number and Operations**
- **Measurement**
- **Geometry**
- **Data Analysis and Probability**
- **Algebra**

D1287750

Provide practice for students working at different levels!

Managing Editor: Cindy K. Daoust

Editorial Team: Becky S. Andrews, Kimberley Bruck, Karen P. Shelton, Diane Badden, Thad H. McLaurin, Debra Liverman, Marsha Erskine, Karen A. Brudnak, Hope Rodgers, Dorothy C. McKinney

Production Team: Lisa K. Pitts, Pam Crane, Rebecca Saunders, Jennifer Tipton Cappoen, Chris Curry, Sarah Foreman, Theresa Lewis Goode, Clint Moore, Greg D. Rieves, Barry Slate, Donna K. Teal, Zane Williard, Tazmen Carlisle, Marsha Heim, Lynette Dickerson, Mark Rainey, Cat Collins

www.themailbox.com

©2006 The Mailbox®
All rights reserved.
ISBN #1-56234-704-7

Manufactured in the United States
10 9 8 7 6 5 4 3 2 1

Table of Contents

Language Arts

Language and Conventions

Word Analysis

Reading Comprehension

Research and Inquiry

Math

What's Inside?

This jam-packed resource contains over 70 pairs of skill-specific language arts and math practice pages. Each pair consists of one practice page that is on grade level and one practice page that is on a lower level, each with the same title and identical or very similar art. To help you easily identify the page you need, the page number for the lower-level reproducible is shown in a black circle.

Same Skill Covered

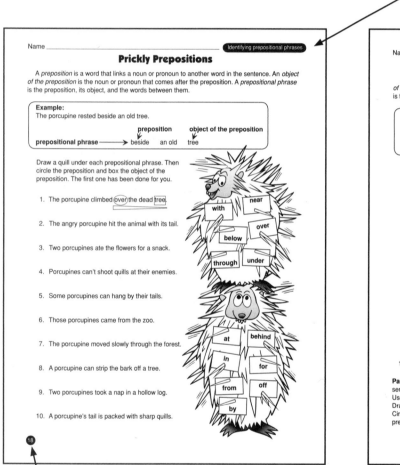

Lower Level Page

Grade Level Page

Circled Page Number Signaling Lower-Level Reproducible

Similar Art on Both Reproducibles

How to Use

Provide differentiated skills practice for your students.

1. Scan the table of contents on pages 2 and 3 to find the skill you need.

2. Determine which practice page best suits your needs, or use both!

Use *Leveled Skill Builders* practice pages for the following:

- small-group practice
- independent practice
- whole-group practice
- remediation
- enrichment
- differentiated homework
- centers
- tutoring

Top-Slice Topics

A *topic sentence* states the main idea of a paragraph. Read each paragraph below. Then, on the top bun, circle the topic sentence that names the subject and gives the main point of the paragraph.

A. Sandwiches come in many forms.

B. Sandwiches are good for lunch.

Sandwiches can be oozing with peanut butter and jelly. They can also be stacked high with bologna and cheese. Some sandwiches are served hot with melted cheese and steak. Sandwiches can come in a pita pocket, without crusts, or on whole wheat bread. Sandwiches make tasty meals.

C. Picnics are good times to enjoy friends.

D. Picnics are enjoyable anywhere and at almost any time.

Pack a lunch, drinks, and a blanket. Then find your favorite outdoor location. Some people like to picnic on the beach or by a lake. You can even picnic in your own backyard. Picnics are especially nice in the spring and fall before the weather is too hot or cold. Picnics are fun events to enjoy with friends.

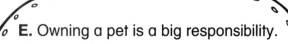

E. Owning a pet is a big responsibility.

F. Pets are a lot of fun.

Pets must have fresh food and water every day. Their bedding must be kept clean. Sometimes pets need to be bathed. You should make sure that your pet gets exercise every day. When a pet is sick, it is important to take it to the veterinarian. Pets need to be loved. Although owning a pet is a big responsibility, pets are a lot of fun.

G. Children should eat healthy foods.

H. Children should eat fruits and vegetables daily.

Children should eat at least three servings of fruits and four servings of vegetables each day. Doctors also suggest eating a diet that is low in fatty foods such as cheese, whole milk, and some meats. Avoiding extra salt and sugar is another way to stay healthy. Eating healthy foods is a smart idea.

Top-Slice Topics

A *topic sentence* states the main idea of a paragraph. Read each paragraph below. Then, on the top bun, write a topic sentence that names the subject and gives the main point of the paragraph.

_____
_____

Sandwiches can be oozing with peanut butter and jelly. They can also be stacked high with bologna and cheese. Some sandwiches are served hot with melted cheese and steak. Sandwiches can come in a pita pocket, without crusts, or on whole wheat bread. Sandwiches make tasty meals.

_____
_____

Pack a lunch, drinks, and a blanket. Then find your favorite outdoor location. Some people like to picnic on the beach or by a lake. You can even picnic in your own backyard. Picnics are especially nice in the spring and fall before the weather is too hot or cold. Picnics are fun events to enjoy with friends.

_____
_____

Pets must have fresh food and water every day. Their bedding must be kept clean. Sometimes pets need to be bathed. You should make sure that your pet gets exercise every day. When a pet is sick, it is important to take it to the veterinarian. Pets need to be loved. Although owning a pet is a big responsibility, pets are a lot of fun.

_____
_____

Children should eat at least three servings of fruits and four servings of vegetables each day. Doctors also suggest eating a diet that is low in fatty foods such as cheese, whole milk, and some meats. Avoiding extra salt and sugar is another way to stay healthy. Eating healthy foods is a smart idea.

Name _____

Delicious Details

Details in a paragraph prove, explain, or support the topic given in the topic sentence. Fill in the blanks with details that support each topic sentence below. Use the back of this sheet if you need more space.

Bag lunches are better than school lunches.

a. _____

b. _____

c. _____

There are good reasons to take a bag lunch to school.

Rock stars lead exciting lives.

a. _____

b. _____

c. _____

It would be exciting to be a rock star.

Pizza is one of my favorite foods.

a. _____

b. _____

c. _____

I love to eat pizza!

A dog can be a wonderful companion.

a. Some dogs play ball with you.

b. _____

c. _____

No wonder some people call a dog a man's best friend.

A field trip is a great experience.

a. _____

b. _____

c. _____

Field trips are a fun way to learn new things.

8

Delicious Details

Details in a paragraph prove, explain, or support the topic given in the topic sentence. Fill in the blanks with details that support each topic sentence below. Use the back of this sheet if you need more space.

Bag lunches are better than school lunches.

a. _____

b. _____

c. _____

d. _____

There are good reasons to take a bag lunch to school.

Rock stars lead exciting lives.

a. _____

b. _____

c. _____

d. _____

It would be exciting to be a rock star.

Pizza is one of my favorite foods.

a. _____

b. _____

c. _____

d. _____

I love to eat pizza!

The kangaroo is an unusual animal.

a. _____

b. _____

c. _____

d. _____

Kangaroos are interesting in many ways.

A dog can be a wonderful companion.

a. _____

b. _____

c. _____

d. _____

No wonder some people call a dog a man's best friend.

A field trip is a great experience.

a. _____

b. _____

c. _____

d. _____

Field trips are a fun way to learn new things.

9

Quick Fix

Write a singular or plural noun to complete each pair of words on the chart. Then tell which rule helped guide your work. The first one has been done for you.

Rule 1

Add *s* to most singular nouns.

Examples:
book—books
car—cars

Rule 2

Add *es* to nouns that end in *sh, ch, x, s,* and *z.*

Examples:
brush—brushes
buzz—buzzes
bench—benches

Rule 3

Drop the *y* and add *ies* if the letter before the *y* is a consonant.

Examples:
city—cities
baby—babies

Rule 4

Add *s* to nouns that end in *y* if the letter before the *y* is a vowel.

Examples:
toy—toys
key—keys

Singular	Plural	Rule
boy	boys	4
	berries	
	pencils	
tax		
monkey		
church		
	wishes	
gas		
	turkeys	
chair		
	skies	
clock		
candy		
	butterflies	

Quick Fix

Write a singular or plural noun to complete each pair of words on the chart. Then tell which rule helped guide your work. The first one has been done for you.

Rule 1

Add *s* to most singular nouns.

Examples:
  book—books
  car—cars

Rule 2

Add *es* to nouns that end in *sh, ch, x, s,* and *z.*

Examples:
  brush—brushes
  buzz—buzzes
  bench—benches

Rule 3

Drop the *y* and add *ies* if the letter before the *y* is a consonant.

Examples:
  city—cities
  baby—babies

Rule 4

Add *s* to nouns that end in *y* if the letter before the *y* is a vowel.

Examples:
  toy—toys
  key—keys

Rule 5

Add *s* or *es* to nouns that end in *o.* Check a dictionary to be sure.

Examples:
  hero—heroes
  piano—pianos

Rule 6

In most cases, if a noun ends in *f* or *fe,* add *s.* In some cases, change the *f* or *fe* to *v* and add *es.*

Examples:
  belief—beliefs
  giraffe—giraffes
  wolf—wolves
  life—lives

Rule 7

The plurals of some nouns have irregular spellings.

Examples:
  child—children
  man—men

Singular	Plural	Rule
boy	boys	4
	berries	
goose		
	pencils	
tax		
	shelves	
veto		
monkey		
	teeth	
knife		
	patios	
church		
	wishes	
half		
gas		
	turkeys	
tomato		
chair		
	skies	
mouse		
clock		
candy		
foot		
	butterflies	
zero		

The Program's Problems

Read the program text. Circle the correct form of the noun in parentheses to complete the sentence.

Plural

A *plural noun* names more than one person, place, or thing. To form a plural, an *s* or *es* is usually added.

Possessive

A *possessive noun* shows that something belongs to a person, place, or thing. To form a possessive, an *'s* is added to most singular nouns and an *'* is added to most plural nouns.

Thank you for coming to this (years, year's) talent show. The (contestants, contestant's)
                                  1   2

are ready to perform. To begin (tonights, tonight's) show, we will recite the Pledge of
                                        3

Allegiance. The (schools, school's) drama club will perform a short skit. After this,
                          4

the (members, member's) of the (boys, boys') choir will sing for us. Then there will be
            5   6

a short intermission. At this time, you may buy (drinks, drink's) and snacks at the
                                                          7

concession stand. After intermission, several (students, student's) will recite a poem.
                                                          8

The (contestants, contestants') names will be read as (awards, award's) are given out.
            9   10

Miss Nora will shake each (winners, winner's) hand. The evening will conclude with
                                    11

refreshments being served in (Mr. Davidsons, Mr. Davidson's) classroom.
                                        12

The Program's Problems

Read the program text. Write the correct form of the noun on the line provided.

Plural

A *plural noun* names more than one person, place, or thing. To form a plural, an *s* or *es* is usually added.

Possessive

A *possessive noun* shows that something belongs to a person, place, or thing. To form a possessive, an *'s* is added to most singular nouns and an *'* is added to most plural nouns.

Thank you for coming to this (1) _____ talent show. The (2) _____ are
                                    year   contestant

ready to perform. To begin (3) _____ show, we will recite the Pledge of
                                        tonight

Allegiance. The (4) _____ drama club will perform a short skit. After this,
                              school

the (5) _____ of the (6) _____ choir will sing for us. Then there will be a
              member   boy

short intermission. At this time, you may buy (7) _____ and snacks at the
                                                              drink

concession stand. After intermission, several (8) _____ will recite a poem. The
                                                            student

(9) _____ names will be read as (10) _____ are given out. Miss Nora
          contestant   award

will shake each (11) _____ hand. The evening will conclude with refreshments
                            winner

being served in (12) _____ classroom.
                          Mr. Davidson

Simon's Simple Signs

Circle the sign text that has correct subject-verb agreement. Write the rule that you used on the chart. The first one has been done for you.

Rule 1
When the subject is a *singular noun* or *he, she,* or *it,* add *s* or *es* to the verb. **Examples:** He walks. Janet sings. He coaches.

Rule 2
When the subject is a *plural noun* or *I, we, you,* or *they,* do not add *s* or *es* to the verb. **Examples:** You swim well. The students run in the gym.

Sign	Sign	Rule
We loves fresh strawberries.	We love fresh strawberries.	2
Good drivers buckle up!	Good drivers buckles up!	
Ice cream tastes great!	Ice cream taste great!	
The bridge freeze before the road.	The bridge freezes before the road.	
We writes messages on T-shirts while you wait!	We write messages on T-shirts while you wait!	
Local runner wins big race!	Local runner win big race!	
Used cars runs well!	Used cars run well!	
I buys old stamps.	I buy old stamps.	
The road curves to the left.	The road curve to the left.	
Mechanic needs assistant.	Mechanic need assistant.	
We sell for less!	We sells for less!	
All vehicles drives slowly around the curve.	All vehicles drive slowly around the curve.	
Dr. Dolan welcome new patients.	Dr. Dolan welcomes new patients.	
Attorney Tommy Thompson fights for you!	Attorney Tommy Thompson fight for you!	

Simon's Simple Signs

Rewrite each sign below using correct subject-verb agreement. Write the rule that you used. The first one has been done for you.

Rule 2
When the subject is a *plural noun* or *I, we, you,* or *they,* do not add *s* or *es* to the verb.
Examples: You swim well. The students run in the gym.

Rule 1
When the subject is a *singular noun* or *he, she,* or *it,* add *s* or *es* to the verb.
Examples: He walks. Janet sings. He coaches.

Incorrect Sign	Correction	Rule
We loves fresh strawberries.	*We love fresh strawberries.*	2
Good drivers buckles up!		
Ice cream taste great!		
The bridge freeze before the road.		
We writes messages on T-shirts while you wait!		
Local marathon runner win big race!		
Used cars runs well!		
I buys old stamps.		
The road curve to the left.		
Mechanic need assistant.		
We sells for less!		
All vehicles drives slowly around the curve.		
Dr. Dolan welcome new patients.		
Attorney Tommy Thompson fight for you!		

Raking Up Parts of Speech

Read the paragraph below. Write each underlined word
on the bag labeled with its correct part of speech.

It was a <u>brisk</u> fall <u>afternoon</u>. The children <u>raked</u> <u>quickly</u> so that <u>they</u>
could get to several <u>houses</u> before dark. The wind <u>whistled</u> loudly. It
sometimes blew so hard that raked <u>leaves</u> flew everywhere. The children
were charging the neighbors a <u>small</u> fee to rake each yard. <u>Everyone</u> had
agreed to use the money for a field trip to <u>Washington, DC</u>. The children
were <u>studying</u> the city in school and desperately <u>wanted</u> to go there for a
visit. Their teacher wanted to go, too. <u>She</u> had visited the city once before.
Several <u>parents</u> eagerly <u>volunteered</u> to chaperone. Raking leaves turned
out to be much <u>harder</u> than the children had previously thought. Maybe
they would have a bake sale next time!

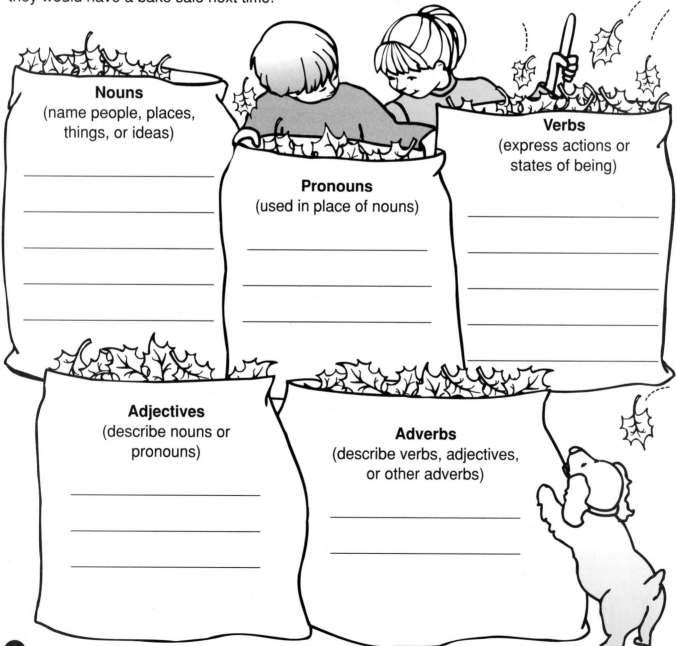

Nouns
(name people, places,
things, or ideas)

Pronouns
(used in place of nouns)

Verbs
(express actions or
states of being)

Adjectives
(describe nouns or
pronouns)

Adverbs
(describe verbs, adjectives,
or other adverbs)

Raking Up Parts of Speech

Read the paragraph below. Write each underlined word
on the bag labeled with its correct part of speech.

It was a <u>brisk</u> fall <u>afternoon</u>. The children <u>raked</u> <u>quickly</u> so that
<u>they</u> could get to several <u>houses</u> before dark. The wind <u>whistled</u> <u>loudly</u>. It
sometimes blew so hard that <u>raked</u> <u>leaves</u> flew everywhere. The children
were charging the neighbors a <u>small</u> fee to rake each yard. <u>Everyone</u> had
agreed to use the money for a field trip to <u>Washington, DC</u>. The children
were <u>studying</u> the city in school and <u>desperately</u> <u>wanted</u> to go there for a
visit. Their teacher wanted to go, too. <u>She</u> had visited the city once before.
<u>Several</u> <u>parents</u> <u>eagerly</u> <u>volunteered</u> to chaperone. Raking leaves turned
out to be much <u>harder</u> than the children had previously <u>thought</u>. Maybe they
would have a bake <u>sale</u> next time!

Nouns
(name people, places,
things, or ideas)

_____

_____

_____

_____

_____

Pronouns
(used in place of nouns)

_____

_____

_____

Verbs
(express actions or
states of being)

_____

_____

_____

_____

_____

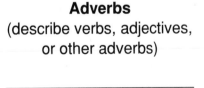

Adjectives
(describe nouns or
pronouns)

_____

_____

_____

_____

Adverbs
(describe verbs, adjectives,
or other adverbs)

_____

_____

_____

_____

Prickly Prepositions

A *preposition* is a word that links a noun or pronoun to another word in the sentence. An *object of the preposition* is the noun or pronoun that comes after the preposition. A *prepositional phrase* is the preposition, its object, and the words between them.

Example:
The porcupine rested beside an old tree.

prepositional phrase ———→   **preposition**
                            beside   an old   **object of the preposition**
                                                tree

Draw a quill under each prepositional phrase. Then circle the preposition and box the object of the preposition. The first one has been done for you.

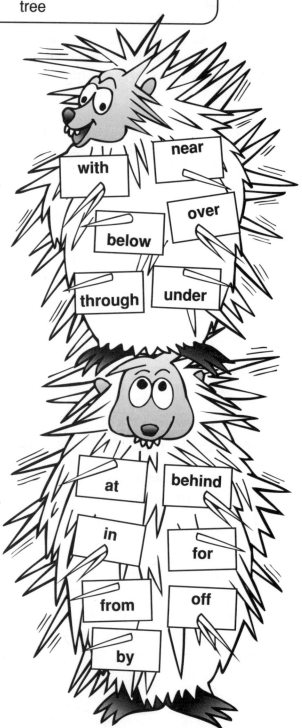

1. The porcupine climbed (over) the dead [tree].

2. The angry porcupine hit the animal with its tail.

3. Two porcupines ate the flowers for a snack.

4. Porcupines can't shoot quills at their enemies.

5. Some porcupines can hang by their tails.

6. Those porcupines came from the zoo.

7. The porcupine moved slowly through the forest.

8. A porcupine can strip the bark off a tree.

9. Two porcupines took a nap in a hollow log.

10. A porcupine's tail is packed with sharp quills.

Name _____

Prickly Prepositions

A *preposition* is a word that links a noun or pronoun to another word in the sentence. An *object of the preposition* is the noun or pronoun that comes after the preposition. A *prepositional phrase* is the preposition, its object, and the words between them.

Example:
The porcupine rested beside an old tree.

                                               preposition   **object of the preposition**

prepositional phrase ⟶ beside   an old   tree

Part 1: Draw a quill under each prepositional phrase. Then circle the preposition and box the object of the preposition. The first one has been done for you.

1. The porcupine climbed (over) the dead [tree].

2. The angry porcupine hit the animal with its tail.

3. Two porcupines ate the flowers for a snack.

4. Porcupines can't shoot quills at their enemies.

5. Some porcupines can hang by their tails.

6. Those porcupines came from the zoo.

7. The porcupine moved slowly through the forest.

8. A porcupine can strip the bark off a tree.

9. Two porcupines took a nap in a hollow log.

10. A porcupine's tail is packed with sharp quills.

Part 2: On the back of this page, write three sentences about the porcupines, Sticky and Pointy. Use a preposition from the cards in each sentence. Draw a quill under each prepositional phrase. Circle the preposition and box each object of the preposition in each phrase.

with   near   over   below   through   under

at   behind   in   for   from   off   by

Stepping Up to Super Sentences

Choose words from the bottom of the page to replace
dull words or add detail to each sentence shown. Rewrite each
sentence in the space provided.

1. Max worked out hard.

   _____

   _____

2. The gym was full of people.

   _____

   _____

3. Music could be heard.

_____

4. She ran on the treadmill.

_____

5. He drank some water.

_____

6. Mindy lifted the weight.

_____

7. Max wore new shoes.

_____

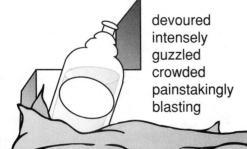

devoured	incredibly	morsel	apparel
intensely	gulped	enormous	comfortable
guzzled	styling	rock and roll	nutritious
crowded	huge	speedily	hoisted
painstakingly	invigorated	refreshing	jam-packed
blasting	bursting	healthy	

Name _____

Stepping Up to Super Sentences

Choose words from the bottom of the page to replace
dull words or add detail to each sentence shown. Rewrite each
sentence in the space provided.

1. Max worked out hard.

   _____

   _____

2. The gym was full of people.

   _____

   _____

3. Music could be heard.

   _____

4. She ran on the treadmill.

   _____

5. He drank some water.

   _____

6. Mindy lifted the weight.

   _____

7. Max wore new shoes.

   _____

8. He ate a snack.

   _____

9. Max has big muscles.

   _____

10. He feels good when he works out.

   _____

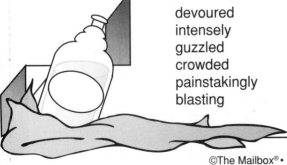

devoured	incredibly	morsel	apparel
intensely	gulped	enormous	comfortable
guzzled	styling	rock and roll	nutritious
crowded	huge	speedily	hoisted
painstakingly	invigorated	refreshing	jam-packed
blasting	bursting	healthy	

Name _____

"Soup-erb" Compound Sentences

When Minnie invites you over for soup, she will tell you to bring just one thing. To find out what it is, follow the directions below.

Directions: Color the soup bowl to show whether the sentence is *simple* or *compound* (two or more independent clauses).

	Simple	Compound
1. Minnie loves soup, and Sid loves salad.	e	a
2. Chicken noodle soup makes a delicious meal.	e	o
3. We use a huge pot to cook the soup.	Y	T
4. The chicken gumbo is spicy, but the rice is bland.	n	p
5. The best vegetables for soup come fresh from the garden.	u	i
6. I'm hungry; let's eat.	g	t
7. The bowls are in the kitchen cupboard above the stove.	p	h
8. It's cold and stormy outside, and I want soup for dinner.	a	o
9. Chicken noodle soup tastes great, but tomato soup is the best.	r	i
10. Don't slurp your soup, or Minnie will give you a straw!	l	r

Write the letter that you colored for each number shown.

___ ___ ___ ___   ___ ___ ___ e ___ ___ t ___ !
3   8   5   10   1   7   4   6   9   2

Name _____

"Soup-erb" Compound Sentences

When Minnie invites you over for soup, she will tell you to bring just one thing. To find out what it is, follow the directions below.

Directions: Color the soup bowl to show whether the sentence is *simple* or *compound* (two or more independent clauses).

		Simple	Compound
1.	Minnie loves soup, and Sid loves salad.	e	a
2.	Chicken noodle soup makes a delicious meal.	e	o
3.	We use an enormous pot to simmer the soup.	Y	T
4.	The chicken gumbo is spicy, but the rice is bland.	n	p
5.	The best vegetables for soup come fresh from the garden.	u	i
6.	Making a big pot of soup can be entertaining, yet eating it is better.	s	t
7.	I'm hungry; let's eat.	g	t
8.	The bowls are in the kitchen cupboard above the stove.	p	h
9.	It's cold and stormy outside, and I want soup for dinner.	a	o
10.	I counted eight recipes for stew in Minnie's recipe box.	e	u
11.	Chicken noodle soup tastes great, but tomato soup is the best.	r	i
12.	Don't slurp your soup, or Minnie will give you a straw!	l	r

Write the letter that you colored for each number shown.

____ ____ ____ ____   ____ ____ ____ ____ ____ ____ ____ ____ !
 3   9   5   12   1   8   4   2   7   11   6   10

Harriet's Handy Helper Service

Harriet's secretary has taken several messages. However, her messages contain run-on sentences. Rewrite each incorrect message on a blank note at the bottom of the page.

Harriet's Handy Helper Service

1. I want to renovate my kitchen I need new appliances and a new floor. Can you please give me an estimate my number is 555-0198.

   (Make into four sentences.)

Harriet's Handy Helper Service

2. Harriet, please come quickly my dishwasher is broken and my suds are filling up my kitchen.

   (Make into two sentences.)

Harriet's Handy Helper Service

3. The wallpaper in my bathroom is peeling please call me at 555-0189. I hope you can fix it soon I am having guests on Friday.

   (Make into four sentences.)

Harriet's Handy Helper Service

4. Do you fix toilets? Mine has been leaking I think the water will ruin the new tile if the toilet is not repaired soon.

   (Make into three sentences.)

Harriet's Handy Helper Service

1.

Harriet's Handy Helper Service

2.

Harriet's Handy Helper Service

3.

Harriet's Handy Helper Service

4.

24

Harriet's Handy Helper Service

Harriet's secretary has taken several messages. However, some of her messages contain run-on sentences.

Read each message. If the message has no run-on sentences, color it yellow.
Rewrite each incorrect message on a blank note at the bottom of the page.

Harriet's Handy Helper Service

1. I want to renovate my kitchen I need new appliances and a new floor. Can you please give me an estimate my number is 555-0198.

Harriet's Handy Helper Service

2. I am calling to thank you for the great job you did repairing my front door. The door is easy to open and never squeaks. I am very happy with your work and will recommend you to my friends.

Harriet's Handy Helper Service

3. Harriet, please come quickly my dishwasher is broken, and suds are filling up my kitchen.

Harriet's Handy Helper Service

4. The wallpaper in my bathroom is peeling please call me at 555-0189. I hope you can fix it soon I am having guests on Friday.

Harriet's Handy Helper Service

5. I need help installing a window. I can be reached at 555-0189 anytime today. Thank you.

Harriet's Handy Helper Service

6. Do you fix toilets? Mine has been leaking I think the water will ruin the new tile if the toilet is not repaired soon.

Harriet's Handy Helper Service

Harriet's Handy Helper Service

Harriet's Handy Helper Service

The Rambling Man

Read each set of directions below. Rewrite the underlined sentence on another sheet of paper to correct the errors.

Egg Coloring Kit

Fill a pan with water. Hard-boil eggs in the water and let the eggs cool. <u>Drop one color tablet into a small amount of vinegar and mix until dissolved and add a cup of cold water.</u> Lower an egg into the colored water and wait until it is the color you desire. Leave it in the solution longer for a brighter color. Drain and place the eggs in a tray. Leave them in the tray until they are completely dry.

Jam and Jelly Canning Kit

This wax is perfect for sealing jars, using in open-topped containers, and making candles. To use the wax in preserving your jams and jellies, fill glasses or jars to within one-half inch of the top. <u>Clean the inside top rim of the container and while the contents are hot, cover with a ⅛-inch layer of melted wax and when the contents have cooled, add another layer of melted wax and tilt and rotate the jar to seal it completely.</u>

Easy-to-Assemble Table

Remove the table from the box. Remove the plastic cover that covers the table and throw it away. Place the table on a smooth surface so that the legs are facing you. Lift one leg up and firmly move the leg until it meets the table at a 90-degree angle. You will hear it snap into place. Repeat this process with the other three legs. <u>Flip the table so the legs meet the floor and the flat surface faces the ceiling and press firmly on the table to test its strength before placing heavy objects on it.</u>

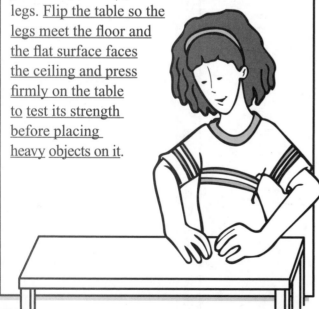

Name _____

The Rambling Man

Read each set of directions below. Rewrite each one on another sheet of paper to correct the errors.

Egg Coloring Kit

Fill a pan with water and boil the water and hard-boil eggs in the water and let the eggs cool. Drop one color tablet into a small amount of vinegar and mix until dissolved and add a cup of cold water. Lower an egg into the colored water and wait until it is the color you desire and leave it in the solution longer for a brighter color. Drain and place the eggs in a tray and leave them in the tray until they are completely dry.

Jam and Jelly Canning Kit

This wax is perfect for sealing jars and it is perfect for using in open-topped containers and it is great for making candles. To use the wax in preserving your jams and jellies, fill glasses or jars to within one-half inch of the top. Clean the inside top rim of the container and while the contents are hot, cover with a $\frac{1}{8}$-inch layer of melted wax and when the contents have cooled, add another layer of melted wax and tilt and rotate the jar to seal it completely.

Easy-to-Assemble Table

Remove the table from the box and remove the plastic cover that covers the table and throw away the plastic. Place the table on a smooth surface so that the legs are facing you and lift one leg up and firmly move the leg until it meets the table at a 90-degree angle and you hear it snap into place. Repeat this process with the other three legs. Flip the table so the legs meet the floor and the flat surface faces the ceiling and press firmly on the table to test its strength before placing heavy objects on it.

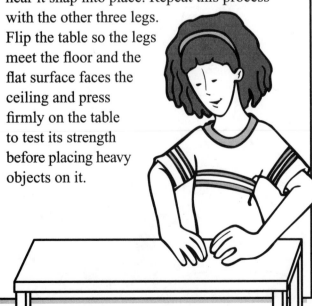

The Capitalization Caper

Help Detective Dogsworth. Color each footprint that contains a word (or words) that should be capitalized. Then rearrange the letters located on the heels of the colored footprints to help him find out what was following Mrs. Hounderson in the park.

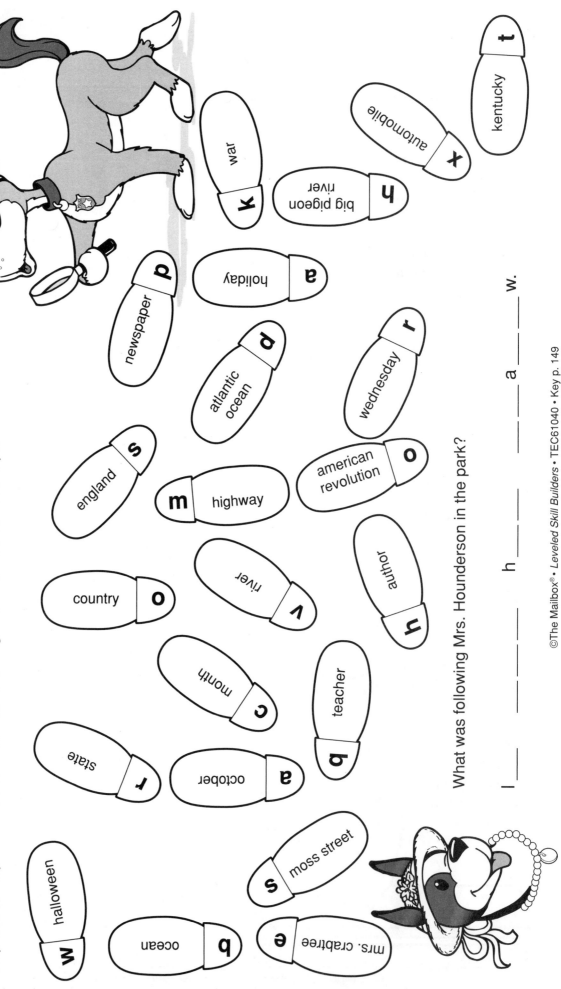

kentucky — **t**

automobile — **x**

big pigeon river — **h**

war — **k**

holiday — **a**

newspaper — **p**

atlantic ocean — **d**

wednesday — **r**

england — **s**

highway — **m**

american revolution — **o**

author — **h**

country — **o**

river — **v**

month — **c**

teacher — **b**

state — **r**

october — **a**

halloween — **w**

ocean — **b**

mrs. crabtree — **e**

moss street — **s**

What was following Mrs. Hounderson in the park?

l __ __ __ __ __ h __ __ __ a __ __ w.

28

The Capitalization Caper

Help Detective Dogsworth. Color each footprint that contains a word (or words) that should be capitalized. Then rearrange the letters located on the heels of the colored footprints to help him find out what was following Mrs. Hounderson in the park.

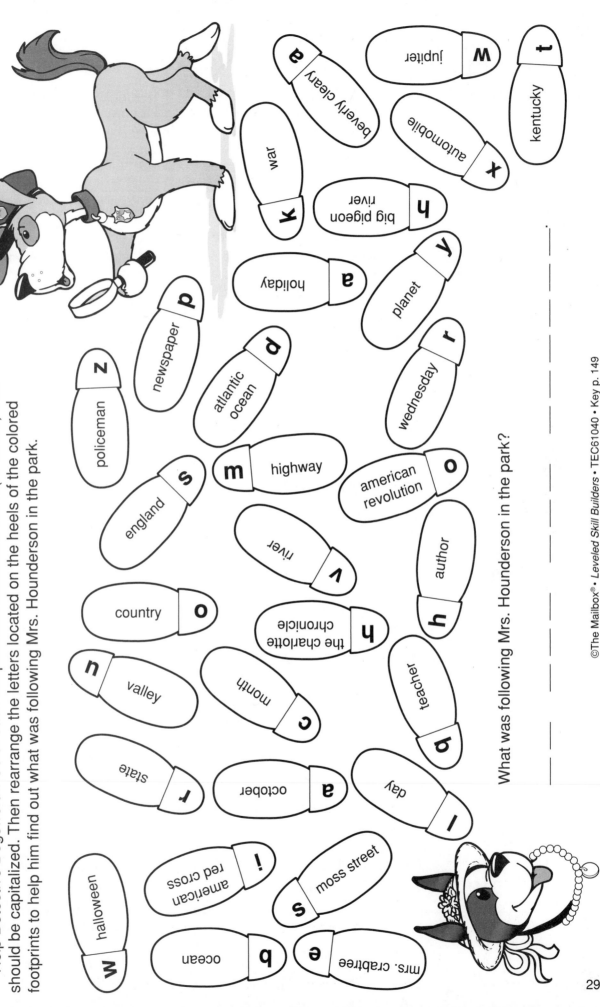

What was following Mrs. Hounderson in the park?

_ _ _ _ _ _ _ _ _ _ _ _

Name _____

With Good Reason

Use the editor's symbol ⌃ to add commas where they are needed. For each sentence, tell why you added a comma by writing the rule number in the blank. If no comma is needed, write "NC."

Rules
1. To separate three or more items in a series
2. Before a conjunction that joins the independent clauses in a compound sentence

Rule Number

🏫 Welcome! 🏫

_____ 1. Welcome back to another school year at Oddville Elementary!

_____ 2. We have much to look forward to in the next ten months.

_____ 3. We have added four new elective classes two new teachers and three new clubs.

_____ 4. We are sad that Mr. Milligan retired but we welcome a new teacher in his place.

_____ 5. We have improved our lunch program by adding ice cream to every menu and we have added comfortable new padded stools to the lunchroom tables.

_____ 6. Our playground has received a new coat of paint on all the old equipment and we have added a state-of-the-art skateboard park!

_____ 7. Our teachers and staff are rested and eager to work with parents and students this year.

 ## Supply List

_____ 8. Each student is required to bring his or her own supplies to class on the first day of school.

_____ 9. You will need two green folders with frog pictures on the front six rainbow pencils a blue crayon and scissors.

_____ 10. You will also need an umbrella a funnel a fork a bag of cotton balls two toothpicks and six medium rubber bands.

With Good Reason

Use the editor's symbol ⌃ to add commas where they are needed. For each sentence, tell why you added a comma by writing the rule number in the blank. If no comma is needed, write "NC."

Rules

1. To separate three or more items in a series
2. After introductory words at the beginning of a sentence
3. Before a conjunction that joins the independent clauses in a compound sentence

Rule Number

🏫 Welcome! 🏫

_____ 1. Welcome back to another school year at Oddville Elementary!

_____ 2. We have much to look forward to in the next ten months.

_____ 3. In fact this promises to be our very best school year ever!

_____ 4. We have added four new elective classes two new teachers and three new clubs.

_____ 5. We are sad that Mr. Milligan retired but we welcome a new teacher in his place.

_____ 6. We have improved our lunch program by adding ice cream to every menu and we have added comfortable new padded stools to the lunchroom tables.

_____ 7. Our playground has received a new coat of paint on all the old equipment and we have added a state-of-the-art skateboard park!

_____ 8. Our teachers and staff are rested and eager to work with parents and students this year.

_____ 9. In short welcome back!

Supply List

_____ 10. Each student is required to bring his or her own supplies to class on the first day of school.

_____ 11. You will need two green folders with frog pictures on the front six rainbow pencils a blue crayon and scissors.

_____ 12. You will also need an umbrella a funnel a fork a bag of cotton balls two toothpicks and six medium rubber bands.

May I Quote You on That?

Underline the exact words that each person is saying. Then add quotation marks.

Quotation Rules

Use quotation marks before and after a direct quotation. Think of them as helping hands that hold a speaker's exact words. To help you know where to put quotation marks, try underlining the speaker's exact words first. Then place the quotation marks before and after each underlined part.

1. Sara said, I think we should allow students to attend school over the Internet.

2. Taking a card from the suggestion box, Tara said, A fifth grader suggests that we start school later in the day. He thinks ten o'clock would be a good time to start.

3. Mark said, We should be able to buy soft drinks at lunch.

4. Marla added, My dad is a nutritionist, and it would be a good idea for students to have a mid-morning and a mid-afternoon snack each day.

5. When it was her turn to speak, Candi said, I think a pet-obedience elective class would be awesome.

6. My mom thinks it would be a good idea if the school buses took kids straight to soccer practice in the afternoon, added Lydia.

7. I agree with your suggestion, said Randall.

8. We should have more time during class to work on homework and projects so our afternoons are free, offered Louise.

9. Sara said, I think we should have sofas and comfortable chairs added to the lunchroom for relaxing after we eat.

10. At the end of the meeting, Kayla said, I don't think we should make any changes. I like school just the way it is.

May I Quote You on That?

Part 1: Underline the exact words that each person is saying. Then add quotation marks.

SUGGESTION BOX

Quotation Rules

Use quotation marks before and after a direct quotation. Think of them as helping hands that hold a speaker's exact words. To help you know where to put quotation marks, try underlining the speaker's exact words first. Then place the quotation marks before and after each underlined part.

1. Sara said, I think we should allow students to attend school over the Internet.

2. Taking a card from the suggestion box, Tara said, A fifth grader suggests that we start school later in the day. He thinks ten o'clock would be a good time to start.

3. Mark said, We should be able to buy soft drinks at lunch.

4. Marla added, My dad is a nutritionist, and it would be a good idea for students to have a mid-morning and a mid-afternoon snack each day.

5. When it was her turn to speak, Candi said, I think a pet-obedience elective class would be awesome.

6. My mom thinks it would be a good idea if the school buses took kids straight to soccer practice in the afternoon, added Lydia.

7. I agree with your suggestion, said Randall.

8. We should have more time during class to work on homework and projects so our afternoons are free, offered Louise.

9. Sara said, I think we should have sofas and comfortable chairs added to the lunchroom for relaxing after we eat.

10. At the end of the meeting, Kayla said, I don't think we should make any changes. I like school just the way it is.

Part 2: Do any of these ideas sound like something you wish your school would do? Choose one of the ideas above. On another sheet of paper, write a conversation in which you and your principal discuss the idea. Use quotation marks correctly.

Say What?

There are two ways to show what someone has said. A *direct quotation* is the speaker's exact words written inside quotation marks. An *indirect quotation* is a statement about what someone said. It does not have quotation marks.

Part 1: Decide whether the following statements contain direct or indirect quotes. Write your answer on the line to the left of the number.

_____ 1. Ms. Payne said that she thinks kids should be able to bring in-line skates to use at recess.

_____ 2. Mr. Horace Norris told the others that we should come to school on Saturday too, just as the children in Japan do.

_____ 3. Mrs. McNeil said, "To save time between classes, why not let the kids use skateboards in the halls?"

_____ 4. Coach Bob Cobb asked, "Can we have a class just for soccer practice?"

_____ 5. Mr. Henry thought letting kids bring their pets to school one day a week would teach responsibility.

_____ 6. "What if we require teachers to take P.E. and let the children have an hour to prepare for the next day's classes?" suggested Coach Randy Dandy.

_____ 7. Principal Garvey said, "Don't you think it would be relaxing to have one faculty meeting each month around the school pool?"

Part 2: These sentences are direct quotations. Add quotation marks in the proper places.

8. I guess it would be a good idea to bring pets to school, said Ms. Marcy Darcy, but who will clean up after them?

9. Miss Kneiss asked, Which class would we drop so that we could add soccer practice? What about the kids who don't play soccer? What class would they take?

10. Principal Garvey said, We'll take a vote at our next meeting.

Name _____

Say What?

There are two ways to show what someone has said. A *direct quotation* is the speaker's exact words written inside quotation marks. An *indirect quotation* is a statement about what someone said. It does not have quotation marks.

Part 1: Decide whether the following statements contain direct or indirect quotes. Write your answer on the line to the left of the number.

_____ 1. Ms. Payne said that she thinks kids should be able to bring in-line skates to use at recess.

_____ 2. Mr. Horace Norris told the others that we should come to school on Saturday too, just as the children in Japan do.

_____ 3. Mrs. McNeil said, "To save time between classes, why not let the kids use skateboards in the halls?"

_____ 4. Coach Bob Cobb asked, "Can we have a class just for soccer practice?"

_____ 5. Mr. Henry thought letting kids bring their pets to school one day a week would teach responsibility.

_____ 6. "What if we require teachers to take P.E. and let the children have an hour to prepare for the next day's classes?" suggested Coach Randy Dandy.

_____ 7. Principal Garvey said, "Don't you think it would be relaxing to have one faculty meeting each month around the school pool?"

Part 2: Identify each sentence below as a direct or indirect quotation. Then, if it is a direct quotation, add quotation marks in the proper places.

_____ 8. I guess it would be a good idea to bring pets to school, said Ms. Marcy Darcy, but who will clean up after them?

_____ 9. Mr. Farrell announced that he is allergic to pets, so he wouldn't be able to attend on Pet Days.

_____ 10. Miss Kneiss asked, Which class would we drop so that we could add soccer practice? What about the kids who don't play soccer? What class would they take?

_____ 11. Ms. Mable Gable pointed out that not all kids have in-line skates or skateboards to bring to school.

_____ 12. Principal Garvey said, We'll take a vote at our next meeting.

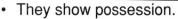

Not Just Hangin' Around

Apostrophes may be tiny, but they have some big jobs to do!

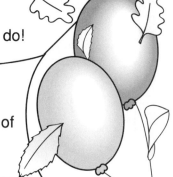

- They show possession.
  The **student's** paper was lost.
- They show that a letter or letters have been left out of a word, as in a contraction.
  Please **don't** turn your assignment in late.

Read about the Fall Festival at Will McGill's school. Add apostrophes where they are needed, using this editing mark: ⱽ. Then color the leaf beside each sentence that needed an apostrophe.

H 1. Will and his new friends arrived early to the schools Fall Festival.

L 2. The booths were set up, and everything was set to go when they arrived.

O 3. First, they went to the art clubs booth to make a scarecrow.

N 4. After a rest and a soft drink, Will was ready to visit other booths at the fair.

W 5. Jan won a prize coupon in Mr. Bumbles balloon-sit game.

D 6. Beau won a prize coupon by making the tallest marshmallow-and-toothpick tower.

E 7. No matter how hard he tried, Will just couldnt seem to win a prize.

O 8. Will and Jan had fun in the P.E. teachers Old Clothes Relay.

K 9. He had a great time at the pumpkin seed–spitting booth, but he still didnt win a prize.

T 10. He came in second in a game of balloon golf, the last game they played.

I 11. At the end of the evening, Jan and Beau redeemed their prize coupons.

Unscramble the letters inside the colored leaves to discover Jan's and Beau's "prize."

Extra

___ ___ M ___ ___ R ___

for one week!

Name _____

Not Just Hangin' Around

Apostrophes may be tiny, but they have some big jobs to do!

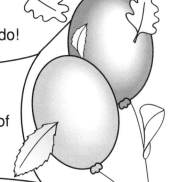

- They show possession.
  The **student's** paper was lost.
- They show that a letter or letters have been left out of a word, as in a contraction.
  Please **don't** turn your assignment in late.

Read about the Fall Festival at Will McGill's school. Add apostrophes where they are needed, using this editing mark: ˇ. Then color the leaf beside each sentence that needed an apostrophe.

H 1. Will and his new friends arrived early to the schools Fall Festival.

L 2. The booths were set up, and everything was set to go when they arrived.

O 3. First, they went to the art clubs booth to make a scarecrow.

R 4. Wills stomach did a flip when he saw a spider on the floor!

N 5. After a rest and a soft drink, Will was ready to visit other booths at the fair.

W 6. Jan won a prize coupon in Mr. Bumbles balloon-sit game.

D 7. Beau won a prize coupon by making the tallest marshmallow-and-toothpick tower.

E 8. No matter how hard he tried, Will just couldnt seem to win a prize.

O 9. Will and Jan had fun in the P.E. teachers Old Clothes Relay.

K 10. He had a great time at the pumpkin seed–spitting booth, but he still didnt win a prize.

T 11. He came in second in a game of balloon golf, the last game they played.

I 12. At the end of the evening, Jan and Beau redeemed their prize coupons.

M 13. After that, Will decided that just hangin around and having a good time was the best prize of all!

Unscramble the letters inside the colored leaves to discover Jan's and Beau's "prize."

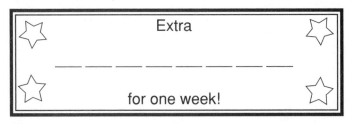

Extra

____ ____ ____ ____ ____ ____ ____ ____ ____

for one week!

Punctuation Repair

Use the editing marks below to correct the letter.

c̲̲	$\overset{.~~.~~.~~.}{\underset{.~~.~~.~~.}{(~~~~~~~~)}}$	$\overset{\bigodot~\textcircled{?}~\textcircled{!}}{\wedge~~\wedge~~\wedge}$
Capitalize this letter.		Insert this end punctuation.

Dear tim,

   how are you I am finally all settled in at our new house. it is smaller than our old one, but at least it has a pool

   i am getting used to my new school. My teacher's name is Ms. sherry berry, and she is very nice. There are 22 other kids in my class I have two new friends their names are Beau Monroe and Jan Haversham. We are in dogsledding class together.

   We have some class pets. We have two fish, some crickets, a baby porcupine, and a ten-foot-long python. It was hard to concentrate at first with Pal slithering around on the floor He's pretty friendly though, so I hardly notice him now. I just try not to drop my pencil

   That's about all the news I have for now. My speed-typing club meets every Thursday, so I'll type you again soon. Tell everyone hello and write soon.

                          Your friend,
                          Will McGill

Punctuation Repair

Use the editing marks below to correct the letter.

c̳	.⌃ ?⌃ !⌃	⌃'
Capitalize this letter.	Insert this end punctuation.	Insert a comma here.

Dear tim

how are you I am finally all settled in at our new house. it is smaller than our old one but at least it has a pool

i am getting used to my new school. My teacher's name is Ms. sherry berry and she is very nice. There are 22 other kids in my class I have two new friends their names are Beau Monroe and Jan Haversham. We are in dogsledding class together.

We have some class pets. We have two fish some crickets a baby porcupine and a ten-foot-long python. It was hard to concentrate at first with Pal slithering around on the floor He's pretty friendly though so I hardly notice him now. I just try not to drop my pencil

That's about all the news I have for now. My speed-typing club meets every Thursday, so I'll type you again soon. Tell everyone hello and write soon.

Your friend

Will McGill

Licensed to Repair

Help Marcus repair each word by changing the underlined prefix or suffix. Then write your corrected word on the line. Use the Vocabulary Van below to help you if needed.

<u>im</u>like	enjoy<u>ship</u>	<u>un</u>agree	love<u>ful</u>
_____	_____	_____	_____

<u>de</u>wind	<u>sub</u>man	child<u>able</u>	happy<u>less</u>
_____	_____	_____	_____

joy<u>able</u>	<u>non</u>courage	cheer<u>age</u>	<u>ex</u>prove
_____	_____	_____	_____

thank<u>ish</u>	hope<u>fy</u>	kind<u>ist</u>	move<u>ness</u>
_____	_____	_____	_____

Prefixes
dis- (apart from, not)
re- (again)
fore- (in front)
super- (over)
over- (over)
un- (not)

Suffixes
-er (one who, that which)
-able (tending to, able to)
-ment (action or process)
-hood (state or period of time)
-ish (having nature of)
-less (without)
-ly (in the manner of)
-ful (full of)
-ness (state of being)
-ous (having the quality of)
-est (most)

VOCABULARY VAN

©The Mailbox® • *Leveled Skill Builders* • TEC61040 • Key p. 151

Licensed to Repair

Help Marcus repair each word by changing the underlined prefix or suffix.
Then write your corrected word on the line. Use the Vocabulary Van below to
help you if needed.

teach<u>ary</u> _____	enjoy<u>ship</u> _____	<u>un</u>agree _____	<u>anti</u>act _____
<u>im</u>like _____	<u>sub</u>man _____	child<u>able</u> _____	love<u>ful</u> _____
<u>de</u>wind _____	<u>co</u>port _____	cheer<u>age</u> _____	happy<u>less</u> _____
joy<u>able</u> _____	<u>de</u>do _____	work<u>hood</u> _____	read<u>ment</u> _____
thank<u>ish</u> _____	<u>non</u>courage _____	kind<u>ist</u> _____	<u>ex</u>prove _____
<u>ir</u>create _____	hope<u>fy</u> _____	<u>inter</u>press _____	move<u>ness</u> _____

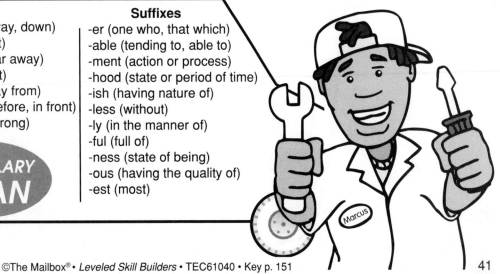

Prefixes

dis- (apart from, not)   de- (away, down)
counter- (against)   im- (not)
ex- (from)   tele- (far away)
re- (again)   un- (not)
trans- (across)   a- (away from)
auto- (self)   pro- (before, in front)
fore- (in front)   mis- (wrong)
super- (over)
over- (over)

Suffixes

-er (one who, that which)
-able (tending to, able to)
-ment (action or process)
-hood (state or period of time)
-ish (having nature of)
-less (without)
-ly (in the manner of)
-ful (full of)
-ness (state of being)
-ous (having the quality of)
-est (most)

VOCABULARY VAN

Time for a Tune-Up

Marcus's new radio commercial contains weak, overused words. Use the word banks to find a synonym for each underlined word. Then write each synonym on the line.

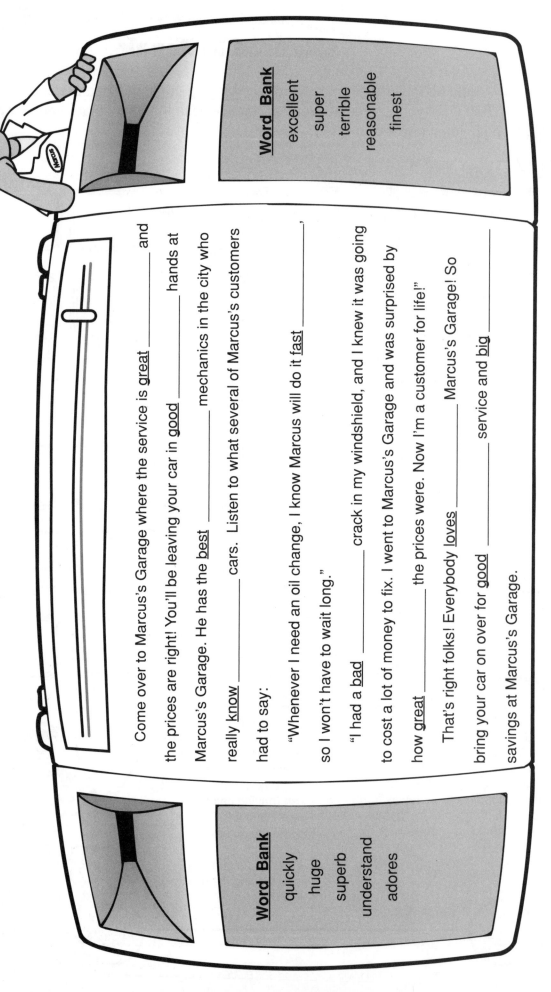

Word Bank

excellent
super
terrible
reasonable
finest

Come over to Marcus's Garage where the service is <u>great</u> _____ and

the prices are right! You'll be leaving your car in <u>good</u> _____ hands at

Marcus's Garage. He has the <u>best</u> _____ mechanics in the city who

really <u>know</u> _____ cars. Listen to what several of Marcus's customers

had to say:

"Whenever I need an oil change, I know Marcus will do it <u>fast</u> _____,

so I won't have to wait long."

"I had a <u>bad</u> _____ crack in my windshield, and I knew it was going

to cost a lot of money to fix. I went to Marcus's Garage and was surprised by

how <u>great</u> _____ the prices were. Now I'm a customer for life!"

That's right folks! Everybody <u>loves</u> _____ Marcus's Garage! So

bring your car on over for <u>good</u> _____ service and <u>big</u> _____

savings at Marcus's Garage.

Word Bank

quickly
huge
superb
understand
adores

©The Mailbox® • *Leveled Skill Builders* • TEC61040 • Key p. 151

Name

Time for a Tune-Up

Marcus's new radio commercial contains weak, overused words. Use a dictionary or thesaurus to find a synonym for each underlined word. Then write each synonym on the line.

Come over to Marcus's Garage where the service is great _____ and

the prices are right! You'll be leaving your car in good _____ hands at

Marcus's Garage. He has the best _____ mechanics in the city who

really know _____ cars. Listen to what several of Marcus's customers

had to say:

"Whenever I need an oil change, I know Marcus will do it fast _____,

so I won't have to wait long."

"I had a bad _____ crack in my windshield, and I knew it was going

to cost a lot of money to fix. I went to Marcus's Garage and was surprised by

how great _____ the prices were. Now I'm a customer for life!"

That's right folks! Everybody loves _____ Marcus's Garage! So

bring your car on over for good _____ service and big _____

savings at Marcus's Garage.

©The Mailbox® • Leveled Skill Builders • TEC61040 • Key p. 151

43

Mixed-Up Mechanic

Read the vocabulary words on each car. Use a dictionary or thesaurus to help you find the matching antonyms on the tires. Cut out the tires. Glue each tire to its matching car.

1. confidential — public or proceed
2. nuisance — agitate or pleasure

3. strict — decorate or lenient
4. appall — assure or lament

5. deface — decorate or pleasure
6. rejoice — lament or desirable

7. polite — idle or uncouth
8. wealth — scarcity or public

9. busy — lenient or idle
10. pause — assure or proceed

11. calm — agitate or scarcity
12. horrible — uncouth or desirable

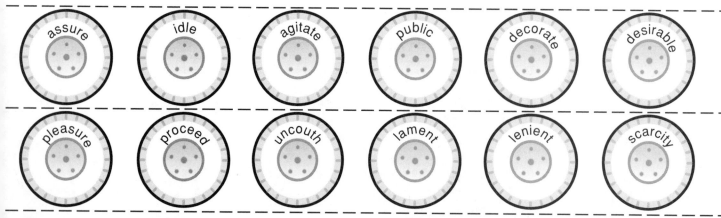

assure   idle   agitate   public   decorate   desirable

pleasure   proceed   uncouth   lament   lenient   scarcity

Mixed-Up Mechanic

Read the vocabulary words on each car. Use a dictionary or thesaurus to help you find the matching antonyms on the tires. Cut out the tires. Glue each tire to its matching car.

1. confidential
2. nuisance
3. strict
4. appall
5. deface
6. rejoice
7. polite
8. wealth
9. busy
10. pause
11. calm
12. horrible

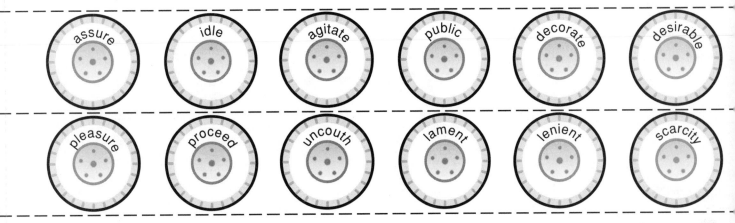

assure   idle   agitate   public   decorate   desirable

pleasure   proceed   uncouth   lament   lenient   scarcity

Crossword Conundrum

Find two clues for each word in the puzzle. Write the number of the word and "A" for across or "D" for down. The first one has been done for you.

The crossword grid:

			³V	
¹B	A	N	K	
O		²A		
W		⁴N	O	L
		C	V	I
⁵F	I	L	E	L
I		O	⁶K	
L		C	I	
E		R	⁷D	A	T	E

___ a place to keep money

___ a tool used to make something smooth

___ a young boy or girl

___ something that hides

___ a certain day, month, or year

___ to gather in a crowd

___ to hold in place

___ a mound

___ a long book with a made-up story

3 D a material that covers the face or head

___ a group of one kind of animal

___ to bend low as a sign of respect

___ the front of a ship

___ new or unusual

___ a get-together with a friend

___ to tease or joke

___ a box or folder that keeps papers

___ a weight used to keep a ship in place

Name _____

Crossword Conundrum

Find two clues for each word in the puzzle. Write the number of the word and "A" for across or "D" for down. The first one has been done for you.

	B	A	N	K				
O		²A						
W		⁴N	O	³V	E	L		
			C	I				
			H	L				
⁵F	L	O	C	K				
	I		⁶K				⁷S	
	R		⁸D	A	T	E		
⁹P	E	A	K					
	¹⁰G	O	A	L				

(Grid letters: ¹BANK across, ¹BOW down, ²A, ³VILL / NOVEL, ⁴NOCH / FLOCK, ⁵FLOCK, ⁶K, ⁷S, ⁸DATE, ⁹PEAK, ¹⁰GOAL)

3 D a material that covers the face or head

_____ a material used to keep something tightly closed

_____ a group of one kind of animal

_____ a place to keep money

_____ something you work toward

_____ a tool used to make something smooth

_____ to bend low as a sign of respect

_____ a certain day, month, or year

_____ a mammal that spends most of its time in water

_____ a young boy or girl

_____ the best or highest point

_____ the highest part of a mountain

_____ the front of a ship

_____ something that hides

_____ new or unusual

_____ a get-together with a friend

_____ to gather in a crowd

_____ to tease or joke

_____ to hold in place

_____ a box or folder that keeps papers

_____ a net on a frame, used in sports

_____ a weight used to keep a ship in place

_____ a mound

_____ a long book with a made-up story

47

Name _____

Picture This!

Similes and metaphors help a reader form pictures in his mind. A simile makes a comparison between two different nouns using *like* or *as*. A metaphor compares two dissimilar things without the use of *like* or *as*.

> **Examples**
> **Simile:** She is as quiet as a mouse.
> **Metaphor:** She is a mouse sneaking across the bare floor.

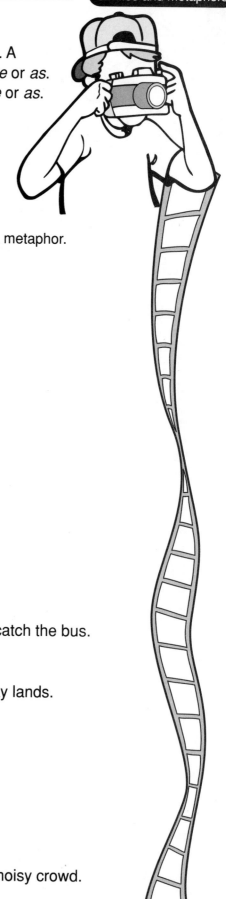

Directions: Read each sentence below and decide if it is a simile or a metaphor. Write "S" for a simile and "M" for a metaphor.

S 1. Monica is as pretty as a picture!

☐ 2. Hannah has a mind like a steel trap.

☐ 3. Lana is a wizard in math.

☐ 4. Jacob was a perfect angel at the party.

☐ 5. Naomi's closet is a junkyard!

☐ 6. Jeremy looked like a speeding bullet as he raced to catch the bus.

☐ 7. This book is like a magic carpet, taking you to faraway lands.

☐ 8. You are my sunshine.

☐ 9. Her evening gown sparkled like a diamond.

☐ 10. Kyle's voice was like a foghorn, piercing through the noisy crowd.

Name _____

Picture This!

Similes and metaphors help a reader form pictures in his mind. A simile makes a comparison between two different nouns using *like* or *as*. A metaphor compares two dissimilar things without the use of *like* or *as*.

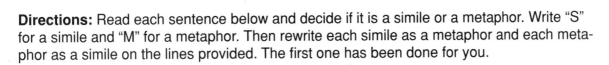

> **Examples**
> **Simile:** She is as quiet as a mouse.
> **Metaphor:** She is a mouse sneaking across the bare floor.

Directions: Read each sentence below and decide if it is a simile or a metaphor. Write "S" for a simile and "M" for a metaphor. Then rewrite each simile as a metaphor and each metaphor as a simile on the lines provided. The first one has been done for you.

S 1. Monica is as pretty as a picture!
       Monica is a pretty picture in her new dress.
       _____

☐ 2. Hannah has a mind like a steel trap.
       _____

☐ 3. Lana is a wizard in math.
       _____

☐ 4. Jacob was a perfect angel at the party.
       _____

☐ 5. Naomi's closet is a junkyard!
       _____

☐ 6. Jeremy looked like a speeding bullet as he raced to catch the bus.
       _____

☐ 7. This book is like a magic carpet, taking you to faraway lands.
       _____

☐ 8. You are my sunshine.
       _____

☐ 9. Her evening gown sparkled like a diamond.
       _____

☐ 10. Kyle's voice was like a foghorn, piercing through the noisy crowd.
       _____

Get the Picture?

Cut out each idiom below and glue it onto the matching frame to complete the sentence.

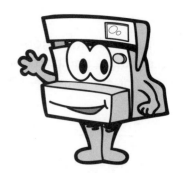

1. Winning second and not first place was
_____
(something to take seriously).

2. Kyle was really
_____
(angry).

3. Daniel, please
_____
(help me).

4. My granny is 80 years old, but she's
_____
(in good health).

5. Sue thought the reading test was
_____
(not difficult).

6. After he got his test score back, Zach looked
_____
(very sad).

7. My brother really
_____
(annoys me).

8. When his sister wouldn't hurry, Joey tried
_____
(not to get impatient).

9. Dillon, if you agree with me, then
_____
(write your signature).

| burned up. | nothing to sneeze at. | down in the dumps. | fit as a fiddle. | gets on my nerves. |
| lend me a hand. | easy as pie. | to keep his shirt on. | put your John Hancock here. | |

Get the Picture?

Cut out each idiom below and glue it onto the matching frame to complete the sentence.

1. Winning second and not first place was
_ _ _ _ _ _ _ _
(something to take seriously).

2. Kyle was really
_ _ _ _ _ _ _ _
(angry).

3. Daniel, please
_ _ _ _ _ _ _ _
(help me).

4. My granny is 80 years old, but she's
_ _ _ _ _ _ _ _
(in good health).

5. Sue thought the reading test was
_ _ _ _ _ _ _ _
(not difficult).

6. After he got his test score back, Zach looked
_ _ _ _ _ _ _ _
(very sad).

7. My brother really
_ _ _ _ _ _ _ _
(annoys me).

8. When his sister wouldn't hurry, Joey tried
_ _ _ _ _ _ _ _
(not to get impatient).

9. Dillon, if you agree with me, then
_ _ _ _ _ _ _ _
(write your signature).

10. When it comes to giving a speech, I always
_ _ _ _ _ _ _ _
(lose courage).

11. To get windows clean, you need to use a little
_ _ _ _ _ _ _ _
(energy).

12. The teacher told Sharon to
_ _ _ _ _ _ _ _
(be silent).

elbow grease.	burned up.	nothing to sneeze at.	down in the dumps.	fit as a fiddle.	gets on my nerves.
hold her tongue.	lend me a hand.	easy as pie.	get cold feet.	to keep his shirt on.	put your John Hancock here.

Much Ado About Movies

Just how are the latest movies doing? Which stars are hot and which ones are not?
To find out, read each review below. Then tell whether it mainly features flick-related
facts or is obviously packed with *opinions*. Ready? Action!

1. *Training Way,* the two-hour film starring Daniel Jefferson, earned $8.6 million in its first three days.

_____

2. The movie *Leaving Home* was tough to follow. The acting was poor and the sets seemed phony. Save your money, folks—don't leave home for this one!

_____

3. *Promising Mabel,* the new comedy featuring Tom Banks and Maggie Ryma, was filmed in Costa Rica. The picture cost $29 million to produce. It opens Friday in New York.

_____

4. Make yourself a vow to go see *Promising Mabel* this weekend! It's funny, warm, and so interesting. You'll want to see it twice.

_____

5. The Motion Picture Agency announced today that the animated film *Best Friends* has been nominated for an Olivia Award.

_____

6. The film *Where Were You?* has won 11 Film Choice Awards. This officially makes the picture the most decorated film in the last ten years.

_____

Much Ado About Movies

Just how are the latest movies doing? Which stars are hot and which ones are not?
To find out, read each review below. Then tell whether it mainly features flick-related
facts or is obviously packed with *opinions*. Ready? Action!

1. *Training Way,* the two-hour film starring Daniel Jefferson, earned $8.6 million in its first three days.

_____

2. The movie *Leaving Home* was tough to follow. The acting was poor and the sets seemed phony. Save your money, folks—don't leave home for this one!

_____

3. Eddie Humpry and Roberto DeNada were paid a combined $60 million for the new movie *Game Time*. Since opening last Wednesday, the film has made over $300 million.

_____

4. *Promising Mabel,* the new comedy featuring Tom Banks and Maggie Ryma, was filmed in Costa Rica. The picture cost $29 million to produce. It opens Friday in New York.

_____

5. Make yourself a vow to go see *Promising Mabel* this weekend! It's funny, warm, and so interesting. You'll want to see it twice.

_____

6. Run for your lives! *Tidal Wave* is coming to theaters! This film has not yet been rated. It took over three years to produce. It came in at $40 million over budget. It opens Friday.

_____

7. *The World vs. Tipton* is the story of a boxer who goes against the world. While I was interested in learning about Marcus Tipton's life, I thought this movie was a waste of my time and money.

_____

8. The Motion Picture Agency announced today that the animated film *Best Friends* has been nominated for an Olivia Award.

_____

9. The film *Where Were You?* has won 11 Film Choice Awards. This officially makes the picture the most decorated film in the last ten years.

_____

Name _____

The Reptile Effect

Match each effect to its cause.

Causes

_____ 1. The bearded dragon expands its "beard"—a set of spiked scales around its throat—when it is threatened.

_____ 2. The harmless milk snake has the same coloring as the venomous coral snake.

_____ 3. Reptiles are cold-blooded.

_____ 4. Geckos have small, lightweight bodies and special pads on their toes.

_____ 5. Moving around during the day in the desert heat uses up a lot of energy.

_____ 6. A chameleon can move its eyes in two different directions at once.

_____ 7. Snakes have specially hinged jaws.

Effects

A. They are excellent climbers.

B. They depend on the sun to regulate their body temperature.

C. The reptile looks too big for a predator to swallow.

D. It can hunt insects and look out for predators at the same time.

E. Reptiles in the desert are active mostly at night.

F. Predators are confused and don't attack.

G. They are able to eat prey bigger than their heads.

Name _____

The Reptile Effect

Match each effect to its cause.

Effects

A. They are excellent climbers.

B. They depend on the sun to regulate their body temperature.

C. Many reptiles are on the endangered species list.

D. The reptile looks too big for a predator to swallow.

E. It can hunt insects and look out for predators at the same time.

F. Reptiles in the desert are active mostly at night.

G. Predators are confused and don't attack.

H. They are able to eat prey bigger than their heads.

I. They rid their bodies of extra salt that has been swallowed.

J. They escape.

Causes

_____ 1. The bearded dragon expands its "beard"—a set of spiked scales around its throat—when it is threatened.

_____ 2. The harmless milk snake has the same coloring as the venomous coral snake.

_____ 3. Reptiles are cold-blooded.

_____ 4. Geckos have small, lightweight bodies and special pads on their toes.

_____ 5. Moving around during the day in the desert heat uses up a lot of energy.

_____ 6. A chameleon can move its eyes in two different directions at once.

_____ 7. Snakes have specially hinged jaws.

_____ 8. Sea turtles cry salty tears.

_____ 9. Some reptiles are hunted for food, and others are used to make belts, shoes, and other products.

_____ 10. If caught by the tail, many lizards let their tails break off.

Reptile Recognition

Read Reptile Ralph's presentation. Then compare and contrast alligators and crocodiles. List the underlined facts in the correct section of the diagram.

   If you have to tangle with a toothy beast in the wild, you'd better know a bit about the kind of animal you're facing! You should first know that alligators don't usually like to have humans for supper. They are shy creatures. They would much rather snack on animals like birds, snakes, and rabbits. Even the big fellows prefer a deer or pig to a person. But crocodiles are another story! They are mean hunters that have been known to stalk and eat humans!

   You can look at their physical features to tell which is which. The crocodile has a slender body and a long, pointed snout. The alligator's body is a bit more heavyset. It has a wide, blunt snout. Another clue can be the water you are near when you spot the beast. Alligators almost always live in freshwater environments, like swamps, ponds, and rivers. Crocodiles prefer calm saltwater homes.

   Alligators and crocodiles do have some things in common. Both are part of the crocodilian reptile group. They are cold-blooded. They are most at home in warm climates. They both lay eggs and have scaly skin. Most are a bit awkward on land, but they are masters of the water. Crocodiles and alligators are sometimes called nature's submarines. They can completely close off their noses, throats, and ears when they dive. They are truly amazing animals!

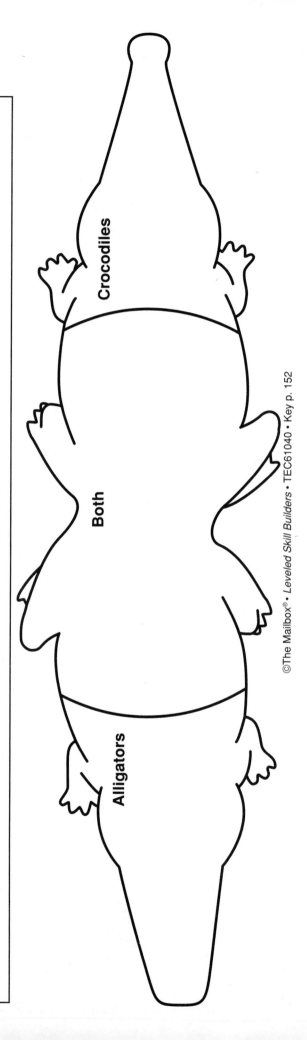

Crocodiles

Both

Alligators

Reptile Recognition

Read Reptile Ralph's presentation. Then compare and contrast alligators and crocodiles. List the facts in the correct section of the diagram.

If you have to tangle with a toothy beast in the wild, you'd better know a bit about the kind of animal you're facing! You should first know that alligators don't usually like to have humans for supper. They are shy creatures. They would much rather snack on animals like birds, snakes, and rabbits. Even the big fellows prefer a deer or pig to a person. But crocodiles are another story! They are mean hunters that have been known to stalk and eat humans!

You can look at their physical features to tell which is which. The crocodile has a slender body and a long, pointed snout. The alligator's body is a bit more heavyset. Alligators almost always live in freshwater environments, like swamps, ponds, and rivers. Crocodiles prefer calm saltwater homes.

Alligators and crocodiles do have some things in common. Both are part of the crocodilian reptile group. They are cold-blooded. They are most at home in warm climates. They both lay eggs and have scaly skin. Crocodiles and alligators are sometimes called nature's submarines. They can completely close off their noses, throats, and ears when they dive. They are truly amazing animals!

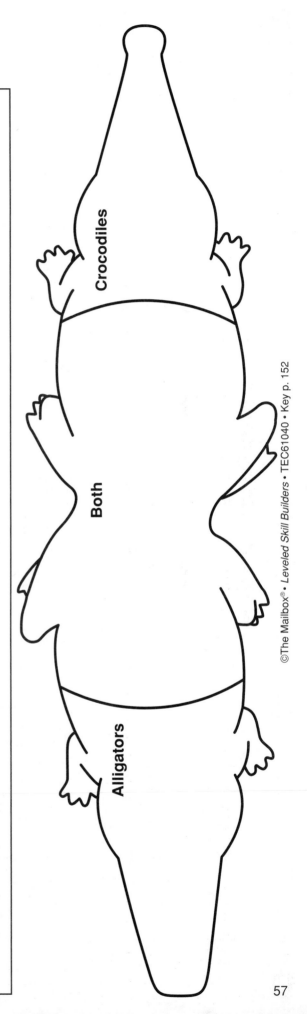

Crocodiles

Both

Alligators

What's the Main Idea?

Poppy Razzi is writing an article about the new actress Starlett O'Hair. Read each of his notecards. Then circle the main idea.

1. She talks to her parents on the phone at least three times a week. While she is filming movies, her five sisters often visit the set. Once a year, the entire family takes a vacation together.

a. The O'Hair family enjoys vacations together.
b. Starlett is very close to her family.

2. Starlett was born in Actorsville. Two years later, her family moved to Setland. When she was seven, another move brought the family to Take Two Town. Starlett lived there until she left to attend acting school. She now lives in Starwood.

a. Starlett has lived in many places.
b. Starlett's favorite place to live is Starwood.

3. At the age of five, she wanted to be a pilot. By third grade, she thought she might be a teacher or own a restaurant. After taking the leading role in a high school play called *Away With the Wind,* Starlett decided to become an actress.

a. Starlett has not always wanted to be an actress.
b. *Away with the Wind* convinced Starlett that she wanted to act.

4. Sometimes she wears her hair piled high on her head. Other times she places feathers, flowers, beads, or silk ribbons in her hair. And, when she's really feeling festive, she might even be seen with a basket of apples atop her head.

a. Starlett enjoys hair accessories.
b. Starlett is known for her fancy hairstyles.

5. She has made five movies, and she is only 22 years old. She says there are many roles she would like to play. She looks forward to playing everything from a grandma to an alien!

a. She hopes to play the part of an alien.
b. Starlett hopes to have a long acting career.

6. She loves to ride horses. She also enjoys hiking and mountain biking. For less active hobbies, Starlett reads and writes poetry.

a. Riding horses is one of Starlett's favorite activities.
b. Starlett has many hobbies.

Name _____

What's the Main Idea?

Poppy Razzi is writing an article about the budding new actress Starlett O'Hair. Read his notecards. Then write a sentence stating the main idea of each.

1. _____
_____

She talks to her parents on the phone at least three times a week. While she is filming movies, her five sisters often visit the set. Once a year, the entire family takes a vacation together.

2. _____
_____

Starlett was born in Actorsville. Two years later, her family moved to Setland. When she was seven, another move brought the family to Take Two Town. Starlett lived there until she left to attend the acting academy. She now lives in Starwood.

3. _____
_____

At the age of five, she wanted to be a pilot. By third grade, she thought she might be a teacher or own a restaurant. After taking the leading role in a high school play called *Away With the Wind,* Starlett decided to become an actress.

4. _____
_____

Sometimes she wears her hair piled high on her head. Other times she places feathers, flowers, beads, or silk ribbons throughout her hair. And, when she's really feeling festive, she might even be seen with a basket of apples atop her head.

5. _____
_____

She has made five movies, and she is only 22 years old. She says there are many roles she would like to play. She looks forward to playing everything from a grandma to an alien!

6. _____
_____

She loves to ride horses. She also enjoys hiking and mountain biking. For less active hobbies, Starlett finds pleasure in reading and writing poetry.

Main Idea Mix-Up!

Cut out the sentences below. Glue each main idea and supporting detail sentence to the correct tent to form two different paragraphs.

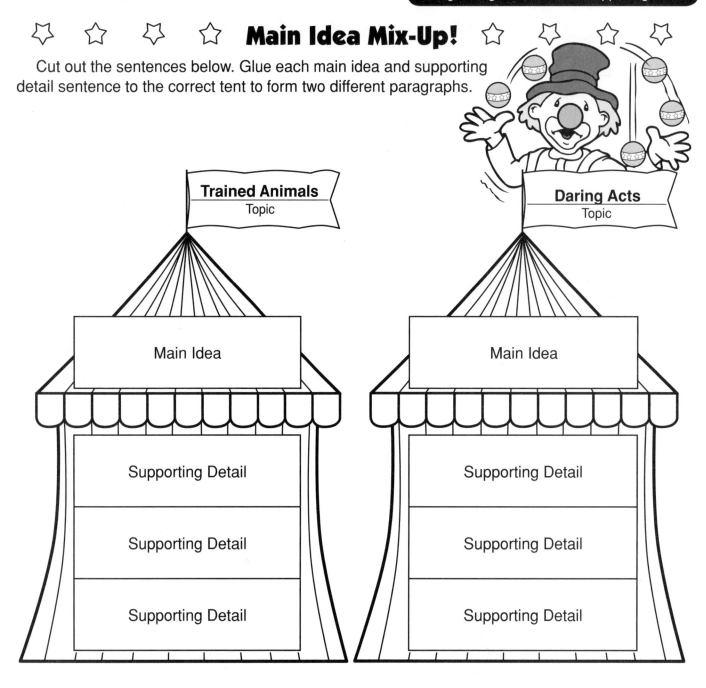

Trained Animals
Topic

Main Idea

Supporting Detail

Supporting Detail

Supporting Detail

Daring Acts
Topic

Main Idea

Supporting Detail

Supporting Detail

Supporting Detail

a. Tumblers entertain with their leaps and flips.

b. Chimpanzees ride on bicycles, and bears jump rope.

c. A circus features daring and sometimes dangerous acts.

d. Tigers are trained to jump through hoops of fire.

e. Human cannonballs are sent flying through the air.

f. High-wire teams perform on a cable high above the crowd.

g. Animal acts are an exciting part of the circus.

h. Performing elephants stand in a line with their front legs on each other's backs.

☆ ☆ ☆ ☆ **Main Idea Mix-Up!** ☆ ☆ ☆ ☆

Cut out the sentences below. Glue each main idea and supporting detail sentence to the correct tent to form two different paragraphs. Then identify the topic of each paragraph and write it on the line. (Hint: One sentence will not be used.)

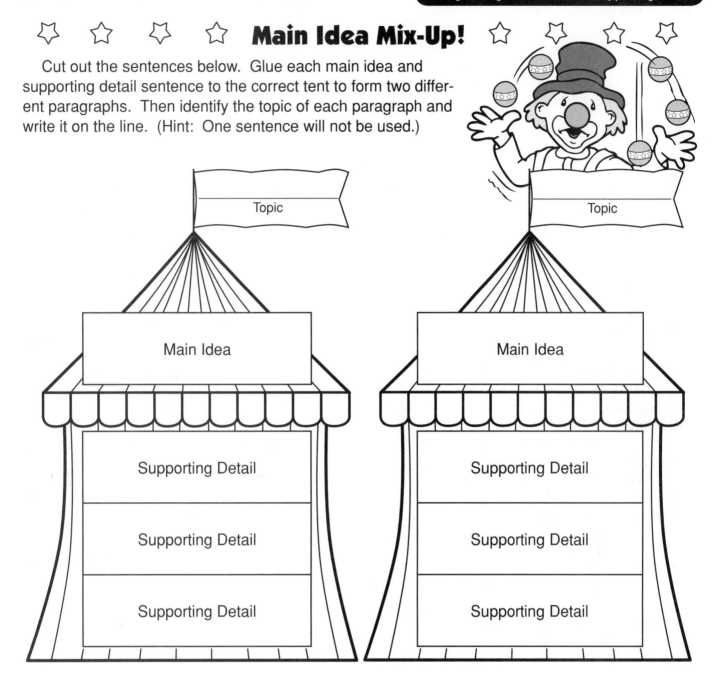

Topic

Main Idea

Supporting Detail

Supporting Detail

Supporting Detail

Topic

Main Idea

Supporting Detail

Supporting Detail

Supporting Detail

©The Mailbox® • *Leveled Skill Builders* • TEC61040 • Key p. 152

a. Tumblers entertain with their leaps and flips.

b. Chimpanzees ride on bicycles, and bears jump rope.

c. A circus features daring and sometimes dangerous acts.

d. Tigers are trained to jump through hoops of fire.

e. Human cannonballs are sent flying through the air.

f. Clowns wear colorful makeup and costumes.

g. High-wire teams perform on a cable high above the crowd.

h. Animal acts are an exciting part of the circus.

i. Performing elephants stand in a line with their front legs on each other's backs.

How About History?

Have you ever wondered how we know about Christopher Columbus's voyage to the New World? Read the passage below to find out. Then complete the questions that follow.

Making History

How do we know about the life of Christopher Columbus? He lived long ago. There were no cameras or computers. Many people could not read or write. Experts look hard to find facts about Columbus. They look in many places.

First, there are some written records. Columbus kept a journal. He wrote about his trip to the New World. He also wrote letters. The king and queen of Spain printed one of his letters. Many people read it. Written records help us know more about Columbus.

Other people wrote about Columbus. His son Ferdinand was on one of his father's voyages. He kept his father's papers and journals. He used them to write a book. Other people also wrote books. These books tell about Columbus.

Finally, there is the public record. About two dozen of Columbus's records have been found. One tells us he was from Genoa, Italy. Another tells us his father's name. A third tells us when Columbus was born. Public records give facts.

Facts are gathered from many places. Experts put the facts together like a puzzle. The puzzle tells us about Columbus's life.

1. Write a sentence summarizing the passage. _____

_____

2. Underline the sentence that tells how experts put facts together.

3. Read the sentences below. Write "T" for true, "F" for false, and "N" if there is not enough information.
   ____ a. Experts can read Columbus's journal.
   ____ b. Ferdinand did not want to travel to the New World.
   ____ c. Columbus was from Rome, Italy.

4. Think about the title of this passage. Do you think it is a good title? Why or why not? _____

_____

5. Circle the letter for the group of words below that best completes this sentence: The author wrote this passage to
   a. get people to like Columbus.
   b. tell how experts research people from the past.

How About History?

Have you ever wondered how we know about Christopher Columbus's voyage to the New World? Read the passage below to find out. Then complete the questions that follow.

Making History

How do we know about the life of Christopher Columbus? He lived long ago. There were no cameras or computers. Many people could not read or write. Experts look hard to find facts about Columbus. They look in many places.

First, there are some written records. Columbus kept a journal. He wrote about his trip to the New World. He also wrote letters. The king and queen of Spain printed one of his letters. Many people read it. Written records help us know more about Columbus.

Other people wrote about Columbus. His son Ferdinand was on one of his father's voyages. Ferdinand kept his father's papers and journals. He used them to write a book. Other people also wrote books. These books tell about Columbus.

Finally, there is the public record. Business matters were sometimes written down. About two dozen of Columbus's business records have been found. One tells us he was from Genoa, Italy. Another tells us his father's name. A third tells us when Columbus was born. Public records give facts.

Information is gathered from many places. Experts put the facts together like a puzzle. The puzzle tells us about Columbus's life.

1. Write a sentence summarizing the passage. _____

_____

2. Underline the sentence that tells how experts put facts together.

3. Read the sentences below. Write "T" for true, "F" for false, and "N" if there is not enough information.
   ____ a. Experts can read Columbus's journal.
   ____ b. Ferdinand did not want to travel to the New World.
   ____ c. Columbus was from Rome, Italy.

4. Think about the title of this passage. Do you think it is a good title? Why or why not? _____

_____

5. Circle the letter for the group of words below that best completes this sentence: The author wrote this passage to
   a. ask for help researching Columbus.
   b. tell how experts research people from the past.
   c. explain how public records are used.
   d. get people to like Columbus.

Change on the Tundra

Read the article below. Then answer each question.
Use the letters after each question to help you find
the answer.

A	Until the 1500s, the Inuit lived off the land with little outside contact. Then European explorers
B	came to the Arctic looking for a northwest passage. They wanted to find a shorter way to the Pacific
C	Ocean. Fishermen from Portugal, Spain, and France came for the cod and herring. Traders were
D	next, hoping to find fox, mink, and beaver furs.
E	Slowly, the Inuit began to trade with the newcomers. Most meetings and trades were friendly, but
F	some were not. Some Inuit were kidnapped and taken back to Europe.
G	In the 1700s, the English, French, and Russians began building trading posts. The Inuit traded
H	sealskin, whale oil, and furs for wooden boats, iron screws, knives, and woven cloth. They used
I	European metal tools in place of the bone and stone tools they had to make. Fishing hooks, nets, and
J	guns made hunting and fishing much easier for the Inuit. To get the European goods, Inuit hunters
K	had to spend more time hunting and trapping. They started trapping animals just for their furs.
L	Over time, the Inuit way of life changed. Whalers came in the 1800s. Some Inuit worked for the
M	whalers. Animals were harder to find. The Inuit came to need the European goods. They began to
N	give up the old ways and move nearer to the trading posts.
O	Besides tools and goods, the Europeans brought disease. The Inuit could not fight smallpox,
P	measles, or the flu. Many Inuit got sick. Thousands died.
Q	The process was slow, but Inuit life changed.

1. From which countries did people come to the Arctic? _____

_____ Lines C, G

2. Why did people from other countries come to the Arctic? _____

_____ Lines B, C, D, L

3. For what did the Inuit trade? _____

_____ Lines G, H, I, J

4. How did contact with Europeans make Inuit life better? _____

_____ Lines I, J

5. How did contact with Europeans hurt Inuit life? _____

_____ Lines K, M, N, O, P

6. Why did the Inuit move closer to the trading posts? _____

_____ Lines M, N

Name _____

Change on the Tundra

Read the article below. Then answer each question.
Write the letter(s) of the line(s) that helped you
answer the question.

A	Until the 1500s, the Inuit lived off the land with little outside contact. Then European explorers
B	came to the Arctic looking for a northwest passage. They wanted to find a shorter way to the Pacific
C	Ocean. Fishermen from Portugal, Spain, and France came for the cod and herring. Traders were
D	next, hoping to find fox, mink, and beaver furs.
E	Slowly, the Inuit began to trade with the newcomers. Most meetings and trades were friendly, but
F	some were not. Some Inuit were kidnapped and taken back to Europe.
G	In the 1700s, the English, French, and Russians began building trading posts. The Inuit traded
H	sealskin, whale oil, and furs for wooden boats, iron screws, knives, and woven cloth. They used
I	European metal tools in place of the bone and stone tools they had to make. Fishing hooks, nets, and
J	guns made hunting and fishing much easier for the Inuit. To get the European goods, Inuit hunters
K	had to spend more time hunting and trapping. They started trapping animals just for their furs.
L	Over time, the Inuit way of life changed. Whalers came in the 1800s. Some Inuit worked for the
M	whalers. Animals were harder to find. The Inuit came to need the European goods. They began to
N	give up the old ways and move nearer to the trading posts.
O	Besides tools and goods, the Europeans brought disease. The Inuit could not fight smallpox,
P	measles, or the flu. Many Inuit got sick. Thousands died.
Q	The process was slow, but Inuit life changed.

1. From which countries did people come to the Arctic? _____

    _____ Line(s) _____

2. Why did people from other countries come to the Arctic? _____

    _____ Line(s) _____

3. For what did the Inuit trade? _____

    _____ Line(s) _____

4. How did contact with Europeans make Inuit life better? _____

    _____ Line(s) _____

5. How did contact with Europeans hurt Inuit life? _____

    _____ Line(s) _____

6. Why did the Inuit move closer to the trading posts? _____

    _____ Line(s) _____

Little Did You Know...

Match each president with a fact. Use the words under each president's name to help you infer which fact fits best.

President

_____ 1. George Washington
"Pearly Whites?"

_____ 2. James Madison
"Feather Friend"

_____ 3. Franklin Pierce
"The Comforts of Home"

_____ 4. Andrew Johnson
"A Thread of Creativity"

_____ 5. Benjamin Harrison
"How Shocking!"

_____ 6. Theodore Roosevelt
"Modern Wonders"

_____ 7. William Taft
"Sleeping Beauty"

_____ 8. Woodrow Wilson
"Nature's Landscaper"

_____ 9. Calvin Coolidge
"Buckin' Bronco"

_____ 10. Franklin Roosevelt
"A Sticky Situation"

Fact

A. Although he installed electric lights in the White House, he never turned them off for fear of electric shocks.

B. On most days, he would ride an electrical rocking horse, whooping like a cowboy.

C. He rarely smiled in public because his teeth were false and made of ivory.

D. He and his wife added modern touches to the White House by installing central heating and a second bathroom.

E. He often took naps while traveling by car.

F. He was the first president to go up in an airplane, go down in a submarine, ride in a car, and visit a foreign country.

G. Weighing only 100 pounds, his friends described him as "no bigger than a half piece of soap."

H. He organized his 25,000-piece stamp collection as a means of relaxing from the pressures of the presidency.

I. He kept a flock of sheep at the White House to keep the grass in order.

J. He made his own suits and was crafty at needlework and quilt making.

Little Did You Know...

Match each president with a fact. Use the words under each president's name to help you infer which fact fits best.

President	Fact
President	**Fact**
____ 1. George Washington "Pearly Whites?"	A. The first pool table was placed in the White House by this president.
____ 2. Thomas Jefferson "Hey, Diddle Diddle"	B. Although he installed electric lights in the White House, he never turned them off for fear of electric shocks.
____ 3. James Madison "Feather Friend"	C. On most days, he would ride an electrical rocking horse, whooping like a cowboy.
____ 4. John Quincy Adams "On Cue"	D. He rarely smiled in public because his teeth were false and made of ivory.
____ 5. Franklin Pierce "The Comforts of Home"	E. He took great care over his appearance and wore fashionable clothes.
____ 6. Andrew Johnson "A Thread of Creativity"	F. He and his wife added modern touches to the White House by installing central heating and a second bathroom.
____ 7. Ulysses Grant "Quite Queasy"	G. He banned yellow from the White House because he didn't like the color.
____ 8. Chester Arthur "In Vogue"	H. He was a talented musician who played the violin daily.
____ 9. Benjamin Harrison "How Shocking!"	I. He despised the sight of blood although he had been in battle much of his life.
____ 10. William McKinley "Whitewashed"	J. He often took naps while traveling by car.
____ 11. Theodore Roosevelt "Modern Wonders"	K. He was the first president to go up in an airplane, go down in a submarine, ride in a car, and visit a foreign country.
____ 12. William Taft "Sleeping Beauty"	L. Weighing only 100 pounds, his friends described him as "no bigger than a half piece of soap."
____ 13. Woodrow Wilson "Nature's Landscaper"	M. He organized his 25,000-piece stamp collection as a means of relaxing from the pressures of the presidency.
____ 14. Calvin Coolidge "Buckin' Bronco"	N. He kept a flock of sheep at the White House to keep the grass in order.
____ 15. Franklin Roosevelt "A Sticky Situation"	O. He made his own suits and was crafty at needlework and quilt making.

Scene Summary

Read each page from a script below. Then circle the sentence that best summarizes each scene.

Scene 1: Jenna moves toward the window. She pulls back the curtains and quickly covers her face. The sky is dark. Trees are bending toward the ground. Leaves and debris sail in front of the window. In the distance, a large funnel cloud can be seen.

Scene 2: Jenna releases the curtains and turns from the window. She runs down the hallway screaming, "Brian, Brian! Where are you?" She enters one room and exits quickly. She moves down the hall and enters a second room. She emerges with a young child in her arms.

Scene 3: Jenna is fighting to stand up in the wicked winds. She has the young boy in one arm as she struggles to lift the heavy door of the storm cellar. Winds are howling. Debris is blowing everywhere. Finally, she opens the door and climbs down a few stairs, then turns and closes the door.

Scene 4: The cellar door opens and Jenna emerges, carrying Brian. Waiting for her are two adults. "Mama! Papa! I was so frightened!" The mother quickly takes Brian, while the father hugs Jenna. After a discussion reveals that no one is hurt, the four walk toward the pickup truck waiting near the barn.

Scene 1

A. Jenna sees a funnel cloud.

B. Jenna looks outside and realizes a bad storm is approaching.

Scene 2

A. Jenna searches for Brian.

B. Jenna runs around the house screaming.

Scene 3

A. Jenna struggles to get Brian and herself to safety.

B. The winds are howling.

Scene 4

A. The family goes home in the truck.

B. Jenna and her parents are happy to be reunited.

Scene Summary

Read each page from a script below. Then write one sentence summarizing each scene.

Scene 1: Jenna moves toward the window. She pulls back the curtains and quickly covers her face. The sky is dark. Trees are bending toward the ground. Leaves and debris sail in front of the window. In the distance, a large funnel cloud can be seen.

Scene 2: Jenna releases the curtains and turns from the window. She runs down the hallway screaming, "Brian, Brian! Where are you?" She enters one room and exits quickly. She moves down the hall and enters a second room. She emerges with a young child in her arms.

Scene 3: Jenna is fighting to stand up in the wicked winds. She has the young boy in one arm as she struggles to lift the heavy door of the storm cellar. Winds are howling. Debris is blowing everywhere. Finally, she opens the door and climbs down a few stairs, then turns and closes the door.

Scene 4: The cellar door opens and Jenna emerges, carrying Brian. Waiting for her are two adults. "Mama! Papa! I was so frightened!" The mother quickly takes Brian, while the father hugs Jenna. After a discussion reveals that no one is hurt, the four walk toward the pickup truck waiting near the barn.

Scene 1

Scene 2

Scene 3

Scene 4

Camping Superstore

Study the ad. Then circle the answer to each question.

1. Which item is not on sale?
   a. flannel-lined sleeping bag
   b. two-person dome tent
   c. camp lantern

2. How many burners does the standard camp stove have?
   a. 1   c. 3
   b. 2

3. Which tents are on sale?
   a. dome tents   c. six-person tents
   b. all tents

4. Each customer can only buy three of which item?
   a. sleeping bags   c. first aid kits
   b. day packs

5. What is not included in the children's clothes sale?
   a. T-shirts   c. socks
   b. jackets

6. What is the sale on backpacks?
   a. 25% off   c. 50% off
   b. $20.00 off

7. What is limited in the hiking boots sale?
   a. sizes   c. styles
   b. colors

8. How much can you save on camp lanterns?
   a. 10%   c. $\frac{1}{4}$
   b. 15%

Camping Gear—Stock Up Now!

All tents are on sale now!

Deluxe two-person dome tent Now $59.00!	Three-person dome tent Now $99.00!	Six-person tent Now $249.00!

Backpack Clearance Sale! Save 50%

Day pack $32.50 (regularly $65.00)
Field pack $40.00 (regularly $80.00)

Sleeping bags for the whole family!

Goose down sleeping bag $219.00

Flannel-lined sleeping bag $55.00

Wool sleeping bag $38.00

Hiking Boots
Your choice $30.00
(Sizes are limited.)

All Camp Lanterns
10% off regular prices

Save 20% on any camp stove.

Standard two-burner camp stove $66.95

Deluxe three-burner camp stove $74.98

First Aid Kits $5.00

(limit 3 per customer)

Save 25% on all kids' clothes!

(Sale does not include socks.)

Camping Superstore

Study the ad. Then circle the answer to each question.

1. Which item is not on sale?
   a. flannel-lined sleeping bag   c. camp lantern
   b. two-person dome tent   d. day pack

2. How many burners does the standard camp stove have?
   a. 1   c. 3
   b. 2   d. 4

3. Which tents are on sale?
   a. dome tents   c. six-person tents
   b. all tents   d. no tents

4. Each customer can only buy three of which item?
   a. sleeping bags   c. hiking boots
   b. day packs   d. first aid kits

5. What is not included in the children's clothes sale?
   a. T-shirts   c. socks
   b. jackets   d. caps

6. What is the sale on backpacks?
   a. 25% off   c. 50% off
   b. $20.00 off   d. two for $50.00

7. What is limited in the hiking boots sale?
   a. sizes   c. styles
   b. colors   d. nothing

8. How much can you save on camp lanterns?
   a. $\frac{1}{2}$ c. $\frac{1}{4}$
   b. 15%   d. 10%

Camping Gear—Stock Up Now!

All tents are on sale now!

Deluxe two-person dome tent Now $59.00!	Three-person dome tent Now $99.00!	Six-person tent Now $249.00!

Backpack Clearance Sale! Save 50%

Day pack $32.50 (regularly $65.00)
Field pack $40.00 (regularly $80.00)

Sleeping bags for the whole family!

Goose down sleeping bag $219.00

Flannel-lined sleeping bag $55.00

Wool sleeping bag $38.00

Hiking Boots
Your choice $30.00
(Sizes are limited.)

All Camp Lanterns 10% off regular prices

Save 20% on any camp stove.

Standard two-burner camp stove $66.95

Deluxe three-burner camp stove $74.98

First Aid Kits $5.00

(limit 3 per customer)

Save 25% on all kids' clothes!

(Sale does not include socks.)

Name _____

It's Your Vote!

Study the chart. Then answer the questions.

National Voter Turnout in Federal Elections
1980–2000

Year	Voting-Age Population	Voter Registration	Voter Turnout	Percent of Voting-Age Population Who Voted
*2000	205,815,000	156,421,311	105,586,274	51.3
1998	200,929,000	141,850,558	73,117,022	36.4
*1996	196,511,000	146,211,960	96,456,345	49.1
1994	193,650,000	130,292,822	75,105,860	38.8
*1992	189,529,000	133,821,178	104,405,155	55.1
1990	185,812,000	121,105,630	67,859,189	36.5
*1988	182,778,000	126,379,628	91,594,693	50.1
1986	178,566,000	118,399,984	64,991,128	36.4
*1984	174,466,000	124,150,614	92,652,680	53.1
1982	169,938,000	110,671,225	67,615,576	39.8
*1980	164,597,000	113,043,734	86,515,221	52.6

*Presidential Election Years

1. Does every person of voting age register to vote? _____

2. Do all of the registered voters vote in every election? _____

3. List three years when the voter turnout was less than 40%. _____

4. Which year had the most registered voters? _____

5. In what year did the greatest percentage of voting-age people cast their votes?

   _____

6. In what years do more Americans seem to exercise their right to vote? _____

   _____

7. How many more people voted in 1992 than in 1982? _____

8. Do you feel all citizens should vote? Why or why not? _____

   _____

   _____

Name _____

It's Your Vote!

Study the chart. Then answer the questions.

National Voter Turnout in Federal Elections
1980–2000

Year	Voting-Age Population	Voter Registration	Voter Turnout	Percent of Voting-Age Population Who Voted
*2000	205,815,000	156,421,311	105,586,274	51.3
1998	200,929,000	141,850,558	73,117,022	36.4
*1996	196,511,000	146,211,960	96,456,345	49.1
1994	193,650,000	130,292,822	75,105,860	38.8
*1992	189,529,000	133,821,178	104,405,155	55.1
1990	185,812,000	121,105,630	67,859,189	36.5
*1988	182,778,000	126,379,628	91,594,693	50.1
1986	178,566,000	118,399,984	64,991,128	36.4
*1984	174,466,000	124,150,614	92,652,680	53.1
1982	169,938,000	110,671,225	67,615,576	39.8
*1980	164,597,000	113,043,734	86,515,221	52.6

*Presidential Election Years

1. Does every person of voting age register to vote? _____

2. Do all of the registered voters vote in every election? _____

3. List three years when the voter turnout was less than 40%. _____

4. Which year had the most registered voters? _____

5. In what year did the greatest percentage of voting-age people cast their votes?

   _____

6. In what years do more Americans seem to exercise their right to vote? _____

   _____

7. How many more people voted in 1992 than in 1982? _____

8. What does this chart tell you about how Americans exercise their right to vote?

   _____

   _____

9. What is your reaction to the information presented in the chart? _____

   _____

   _____

10. Do you feel all citizens should vote? Why or why not? _____

    _____

Name _____

Dictionary Dilemma

Read the guide words on each dictionary page. Cross out the words in the list that would not apppear on that page. Then write the words on that page in alphabetical order in the spaces provided.

1. gamut   garden

_____gander_____

_____

_____

_____

_____

Word List

gander

~~gash~~

garbage

gangplank

gape

gangly

2. sideways   silly

_____

_____sight_____

_____

_____

_____

Word List

silver

silence

sight

silky

silent

siding

3. hue   humbug

_____huff_____

_____

_____

_____

_____

Word List

huge

huddle

hula

humble

huff

hulk

4. mocha   mole

_____

_____

_____

_____

_____moldy_____

Word List

moldy

model

modem

moss

moisture

mohair

5. backstage   balloon

_____badminton_____

_____

_____

_____

_____

Word List

balk

ballet

badminton

ball

backspin

baffle

6. plentiful   plumber

_____

_____

_____

_____

_____plum_____

Word List

pledge

plight

plow

plenty

plot

plum

Dictionary Dilemma

Read the guide words on each dictionary page. Cross out the words in the list that would not apppear on that page. Then write the words on that page in alphabetical order in the spaces provided.

1. gamut   garden

_____
_____
_____
_____
_____
_____

Word List

gander
gash
gangway
garbage
gamma
gape
gangplank
gangly

2. sideways   silly

_____
_____
_____
_____
_____
_____
_____

Word List

sift
silver
signal
silence
sight
silky
silent
siding

3. hue   humbug

_____
_____
_____
_____
_____

Word List

huge
huddle
hula
humble
hullabaloo
huff
how
hulk

4. mocha   mole

_____
_____
_____
_____
_____
_____

Word List

moist
moldy
model
modem
moss
mob
moisture
mohair
mock

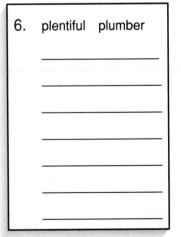

5. backstage   balloon

_____
_____
_____
_____
_____

Word List

balk
ballyhoo
ballet
badminton
ball
backspin
backstroke
baffle

6. plentiful   plumber

_____
_____
_____
_____
_____
_____
_____

Word List

plug
pledge
plight
plow
plenty
pleat
plot
plum
pliers

Unleashing the Meaning

Dig into the dictionary selection below to find a meaning that fits the context of each underlined word. Write the number of the meaning you choose in the bone. The first one is done for you.

bark (bark) 1. to make the short, loud sound of a dog 2. the hard covering on the outside of a tree

chow (chau) 1. food 2. to eat 3. a breed of dog of Chinese origin with a heavy coat, broad head and muzzle, and a black-lined mouth with a blue-black tongue

dog (dawg *or* dog) 1. a domestic mammal with four legs, usually kept as a pet or work animal 2. to follow someone closely

lap (lap) 1. the flat area formed by the top of the legs when sitting 2. one time over or around something, such as a track 3. to drink by flicking liquid into the mouth with the tongue

spot (spot) 1. a small mark or stain 2. an area on the skin or fur that is different from the area around it 3. a place or location 4. to notice something or someone

tick (tik) 1. the clicking sound of a clock or watch 2. a very small animal that attaches itself to the skin of animals or people and sucks blood

SPANKY

2   1. The little puppy <u>dogged</u> his mother everywhere she went.

2. I cannot sleep when the dogs <u>bark</u> all night.

3. The dalmatian is covered with black <u>spots</u>.

4. Spanky curled up on my <u>lap</u> for a long nap.

5. The <u>chow</u> must have been tasty because he ate it all.

6. The little dog sits in the window until he <u>spots</u> his owner's car turning the corner.

7. The puppy heard the <u>tick</u> and was curious as to what was causing it.

8. We decided to buy the beautiful <u>chow</u> from the pet store.

9. Spanky and I ran three <u>laps</u> around the park.

10. Under the big oak tree is Spanky's favorite <u>spot</u> to sleep.

Unleashing the Meaning

Dig into the dictionary selection below to find a meaning that fits the context of each underlined word. Write the number of the meaning you choose in the bone. The first one is done for you.

bark (bark) 1. to make the short, loud sound of a dog 2. the hard covering on the outside of a tree

chow (chau) 1. food 2. to eat 3. a breed of dog of Chinese origin with a heavy coat, broad head and muzzle, and a black-lined mouth with a blue-black tongue

dog (dawg *or* dog) 1. a domestic mammal with four legs, usually kept as a pet or work animal 2. to follow someone closely

lap (lap) 1. the flat area formed by the top of the legs when sitting 2. one time over or around something, such as a track 3. to drink by flicking liquid into the mouth with the tongue

spot (spot) 1. a small mark or stain 2. an area on the skin or fur that is different from the area around it 3. a place or location 4. to notice something or someone

tick (tik) 1. the clicking sound of a clock or watch 2. a very small animal that attaches itself to the skin of animals or people and sucks blood

SPANKY

2 1. The little puppy <u>dogged</u> his mother everywhere she went.

2. I cannot sleep when the dogs <u>bark</u> all night.

3. The dalmatian is covered with black <u>spots</u>.

4. Spanky curled up on my <u>lap</u> for a long nap.

5. The <u>chow</u> must have been tasty because he ate it all.

6. The little dog sits in the window until he <u>spots</u> his owner's car turning the corner.

7. The puppy heard the <u>tick</u> and was curious as to what was causing it.

8. We decided to buy the beautiful <u>chow</u> from the pet store.

9. Spanky and I ran three <u>laps</u> around the park.

10. Under the big oak tree is Spanky's favorite <u>spot</u> to sleep.

11. I called out to the dogs, "It's time to <u>chow</u> down!"

12. Spanky makes a slurping sound as he <u>laps</u> the water from his bowl.

13. The puppy's dirty paws made a <u>spot</u> on the rug.

14. I took Spanky to the vet when I noticed a <u>tick</u> on his back.

15. The new puppy loved to run outside and chew on the <u>bark</u> of the pine tree.

Name _____

A Web of Resources

Look at the resources on the web. Read how each one is used in the space provided. Next, decide which resource is the *best* one to use to answer each question below. Then write the corresponding letter in the blank.

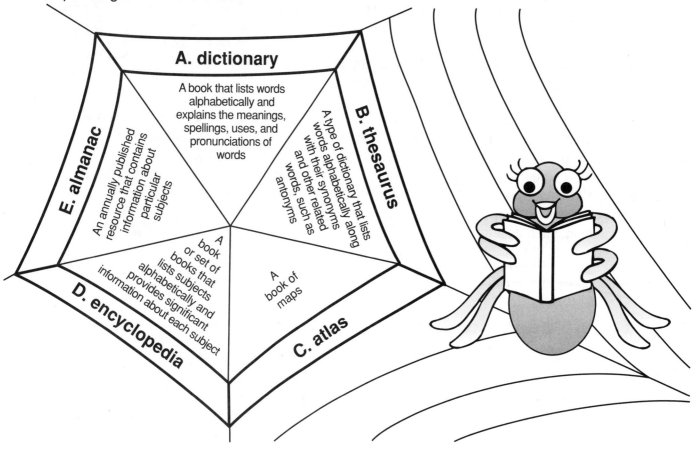

A. dictionary
A book that lists words alphabetically and explains the meanings, spellings, uses, and pronunciations of words

E. almanac
An annually published resource that contains information about particular subjects

B. thesaurus
A type of dictionary that lists words alphabetically along with their synonyms and other related words, such as antonyms

D. encyclopedia
A book or set of books that lists subjects alphabetically and provides significant information about each subject

C. atlas
A book of maps

____ 1. A newspaper article about a new display is titled "Fossilized Figure Ready for Raleigh Museum." Where is Raleigh located?

____ 2. Spinella the spider enjoyed reading an article about the dinosaur. What does the word *fossilized* mean?

____ 3. The fossilized figure was found in Alberta, Canada. What is the current population of Alberta?

____ 4. Alberta is a province in Canada. What other provinces make up the country of Canada?

____ 5. Spinella notices that most of the children who view the display say, "It's huge!" What are some other words that could be used to describe the size of the creature?

____ 6. Spinella learned that the world's leading dinosaur museum is located in Alberta. What are some other interesting facts about Alberta?

____ 7. A paleontologist discovered the dinosaur in 1993. What is the pronunciation of the word *paleontologist*?

____ 8. The museum featuring the new exhibit is located in the state capital of North Carolina. What is the current economy like there?

Name _____

A Web of Resources

Look at the resources on the web. Write how each one is used in the space provided. Next, decide which resource is the *best* one to use to answer each question below. Then write the corresponding letter in the blank.

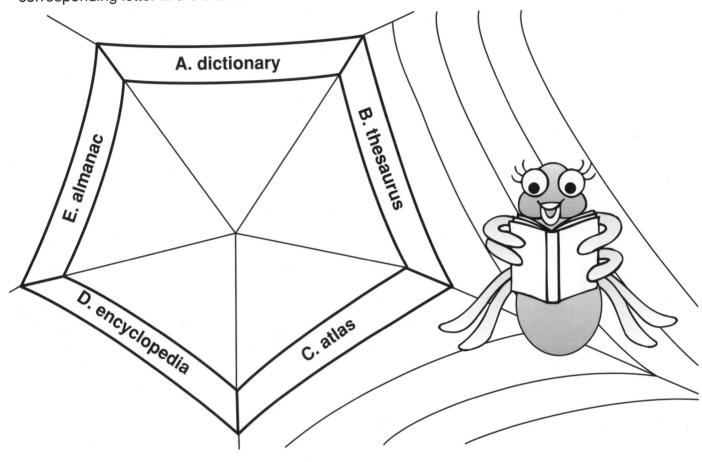

____ 1. A newspaper article about a new display is titled "Fossilized Figure Ready for Raleigh Museum." Where is Raleigh located?

____ 2. Spinella the spider enjoyed reading an article about the dinosaur. What does the word *fossilized* mean?

____ 3. The fossilized figure was found in Alberta, Canada. What is the current population of Alberta?

____ 4. Alberta is a province in Canada. What other provinces make up the country of Canada?

____ 5. The dinosaur on display is a member of the *ornithischian* group. What are some features of this dinosaur group?

____ 6. Spinella notices that most of the children who view the display say, "It's huge!" What are some other words that could be used to describe the size of the creature?

____ 7. Spinella learned that the world's leading dinosaur museum is located in Alberta. What are some other interesting facts about Alberta?

____ 8. A paleontologist discovered the dinosaur in 1993. What is the pronunciation of the word *paleontologist?*

____ 9. Spinella also learned that this type of dinosaur lived during the Cretaceous Period and ranged from Wyoming and the Dakotas northward to Alberta. How far is Cheyenne, Wyoming, from Alberta?

____ 10. The museum featuring the new exhibit is located in the state capital of North Carolina. What is the current economy like there?

Shipping Codes

Determine the value of the 7 in each number. Then look at the chart and write its code on the line.

Place Value of 7	Code
Ones	O
Tens	T
Hundreds	H
Thousands	Th
Ten Thousands	TTh
Hundred Thousands	HTh

1. 976,210
____ Code

2. 903,708
____ Code

3. 864,370
____ Code

4. 895,197
____ Code

5. 784,033
____ Code

6. 870,893
____ Code

7. 580,725
____ Code

8. 271,004
____ Code

9. 557,344
____ Code

10. 506,715
____ Code

11. 301,027
____ Code

12. 397,055
____ Code

13. 106,793
____ Code

14. 507,531
____ Code

15. 784,063
____ Code

Shipping Codes

Determine the value of the 7 in each number. Then look at the chart and write its code on the line.

Place Value of 7	Code
Ones	O
Tens	T
Hundreds	H
Thousands	Th
Ten Thousands	TTh
Hundred Thousands	HTh

1. 976,210 _____ Code

2. 903,708 _____ Code

3. 864,370 _____ Code

4. 895,197 _____ Code

5. 784,033 _____ Code

6. 870,893 _____ Code

7. 580,725 _____ Code

8. 271,004 _____ Code

9. 557,344 _____ Code

10. 506,715 _____ Code

11. 301,027 _____ Code

12. 397,055 _____ Code

13. 106,793 _____ Code

14. 507,531 _____ Code

15. 784,063 _____ Code

16. 238,007 _____ Code

17. 805,722 _____ Code

18. 798,500 _____ Code

19. 905,785 _____ Code

20. 288,537 _____ Code

Slogan Selection

Andrew needs a new slogan to promote his product—the widget. Decide if the place value listed for the underlined number is correct or incorrect. Then color the corresponding box.

Number	Place Value	Correct	Incorrect
1. 54,6<u>0</u>2	hundreds	L	W
2. <u>4</u>98,542	millions	I	M
3. <u>1</u>,438,726	millions	Y	D
4. 2,1<u>2</u>0	tens	P	G
5. <u>4</u>0,903,000	millions	E	P
6. 6<u>4</u>3,008	hundred thousands	T	L
7. <u>1</u>,645,981	ones	S	H
8. 46,<u>6</u>523	thousands	K	R
9. 4<u>3</u>5,876	ten thousands	C	O
10. 8,<u>2</u>64,795	hundreds	C	I
11. <u>2</u>,563,400	millions	E	K
12. 1<u>3</u>7,119	hundred thousands	!	?

Write the letters of the unshaded boxes to reveal the new slogan.

The new slogan is _____

Slogan Selection

Andrew needs a new slogan to promote his product—the widget. Decide if the place value listed for the underlined number is correct or incorrect. Then color the corresponding box.

Number	Place Value	Correct	Incorrect
1. 54,602	hundreds	L	W
2. 498,542	millions	I	M
3. 1,438,726	millions	Y	D
4. 2,120	tens	P	G
5. 40,903,000	millions	E	P
6. 643,008	hundred thousands	T	L
7. 1,645,981	ones	S	H
8. 46,523	thousands	K	W
9. 435,876	ten thousands	C	O
10. 8,264,795	hundreds	R	I
11. 2,563,400	millions	E	K
12. 137,119	hundred thousands	W	X
13. 3,467	tens	O	S
14. 9,530,678	millions	L	N
15. 999,000	hundred thousands	P	D
16. 6,279	thousands	Y	E
17. 4,518	tens	R	P
18. 65,398	ten thousands	S	J

Write the letters of the unshaded boxes to reveal the new slogan.

The new slogan is _____!

Where's My Mummy?

While touring a museum in New York City, Tom and Tina got separated from their mom!
Multiply. Then match each letter to a numbered line below to find out where they found her.

1. 32 × 8 **A**	2. 25 × 7 **E**	3. 561 × 4 **B**	4. 30 × 6 **T**	5. 936 × 3 **Y**
6. 96 × 6 **T**	7. 98 × 5 **N**	8. 715 × 3 **X**	9. 254 × 6 **I**	10. 67 × 7 **H**
11. 87 × 7 **I**	12. 905 × 3 **G**	13. 358 × 9 **I**	14. 47 × 5 **E**	15. 13 × 6 **P**

Where did the kids find their mom?

The ____ ____ ____ ____ ____ ____ ____ ____
235 2,715 2,808 78 180 609 256 490

____ ____ ____ ____ ____ ____ ____ .
175 2,145 469 1,524 2,244 3,222 576

Name _____

Name _____

Where's My Mummy?

While touring a museum in New York City, Tom and Tina got separated from their mom!
Multiply. Then match each letter to a numbered line below to find out where they found her.

1. 32 x 8 **A**	2. 25 x 17 **E**	3. 561 x 4 **B**	4. 30 x 16 **T**	5. 936 x 3 **Y**
6. 96 x 6 **T**	7. 98 x 20 **N**	8. 715 x 23 **X**	9. 254 x 6 **I**	10. 67 x 7 **H**
11. 87 x 21 **I**	12. 905 x 30 **G**	13. 358 x 9 **I**	14. 47 x 5 **E**	15. 13 x 56 **P**

Where did the kids find their mom?

The ____ ____ ____ ____ ____ ____ ____ ____
235   27,150   2,808   728   480   1,827   256   1,960

____ ____ ____ ____ ____ ____ ____ .
425   16,445   469   1,524   2,244   3,222   576

Division Trail

Divide. Then add the remainders to find out how much Tom and Tina spent on souvenirs in New York City.

1 $2\overline{)49}$

2 $5\overline{)85}$

3 $6\overline{)125}$

4 $4\overline{)55}$

5 $8\overline{)308}$

6 $3\overline{)75}$

7 $4\overline{)755}$

8 $8\overline{)168}$

9 $7\overline{)98}$

10 $5\overline{)692}$

11 $3\overline{)109}$

12 $2\overline{)77}$

How much money did Tom and Tina spend on souvenirs?

$ _____

Name _____

Division Trail

Divide. Then add the remainders to find out how much Tom and Tina spent on souvenirs in New York City.

1. $2\overline{)49}$

2. $5\overline{)85}$

3. $9\overline{)292}$

4. $6\overline{)125}$

5. $7\overline{)222}$

6. $4\overline{)55}$

7. $8\overline{)308}$

8. $3\overline{)75}$

9. $4\overline{)755}$

10. $8\overline{)168}$

11. $7\overline{)98}$

12. $5\overline{)692}$

13. $9\overline{)196}$

14. $3\overline{)109}$

15. $6\overline{)911}$

16. $2\overline{)77}$

How much money did Tom and Tina spend on souvenirs?

$ _____

Dining With Decimal Dude

What's for dinner at the Rockin' D Ranch? Color the place value of the underlined digit to show the path. The first one has been done for you.

1. 0.2<u>3</u>	ones	hundredths	tenths
2. <u>1</u>.23	tenths	hundredths	ones
3. <u>5</u>.4	hundredths	tenths	ones
4. 6.<u>2</u>1	ones	tenths	hundredths
5. 0.<u>0</u>5	tenths	ones	hundredths
6. 9.8<u>4</u>	hundredths	tenths	ones
7. <u>0</u>.48	hundredths	ones	tenths
8. <u>1</u>.91	hundredths	ones	tenths
9. 0.<u>7</u>2	ones	tenths	hundredths
10. 1.1<u>3</u>	tenths	hundredths	ones
11. 0.4<u>6</u>	ones	tenths	hundredths
12. <u>7</u>.11	hundredths	tenths	ones
13. 0.<u>2</u>4	hundredths	tenths	ones
14. 0.<u>9</u>8	hundredths	ones	tenths
15. 1.<u>5</u>4	ones	hundredths	tenths

Chuck Wagon Chow

Buckaroo Burger

Ten-Ounce T-Bone

Dining With Decimal Dude

What's for dinner at the Rockin' D Ranch?
Color the place value of the underlined digit to
show the path. The first one has been done
for you.

1. 0.2<u>3</u>3	ones	hundredths	thousandths	tenths
2. <u>1</u>.239	tenths	thousandths	ones	hundredths
3. <u>5</u>.4	hundredths	thousandths	ones	tenths
4. 6.<u>2</u>15	thousandths	ones	tenths	hundredths
5. 0.05<u>4</u>	ones	thousandths	hundredths	tenths
6. 9.8<u>4</u>5	hundredths	tenths	ones	thousandths
7. 0.48<u>3</u>	thousandths	ones	tenths	hundredths
8. <u>1</u>.91	hundredths	ones	thousandths	tenths
9. 0.<u>7</u>23	ones	tenths	hundredths	thousandths
10. 1.1<u>3</u>5	tenths	hundredths	thousandths	ones
11. 0.4<u>6</u>2	thousandths	tenths	hundredths	ones
12. <u>7</u>.11	hundredths	thousandths	ones	tenths
13. 0.24<u>9</u>	tenths	thousandths	ones	hundredths
14. 0.<u>9</u>8	thousandths	ones	tenths	hundredths
15. 1.54<u>6</u>	ones	hundredths	tenths	thousandths

Chuck Wagon Chow

Buckaroo Burger

Sidesaddle Soup

Ten-Ounce T-Bone

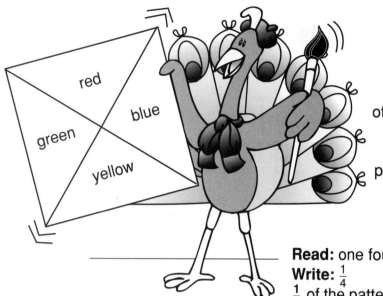

Peabo's Passion

A **fraction** is a number that names part of a whole. The whole represents 1.

parts that are blue→ **1** ← numerator

total equal parts→ **4** ← denominator

Read: one fourth, one out of four, or one divided by four
Write: $\frac{1}{4}$
$\frac{1}{4}$ of the pattern is blue.

Color each shape. Then write a fraction to complete the statement.

(color code: r = red, b = blue, g = green, y = yellow, o = orange, br = brown)

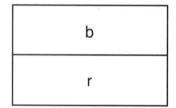

1. _____ is red.

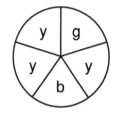

2. _____ is yellow.

3. _____ is not red.

4. _____ is colored.

5. _____ is green.

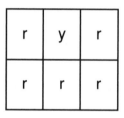

6. _____ is not red.

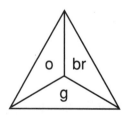

7. _____ is yellow.

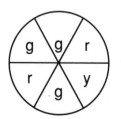

8. _____ is green or red.

Name _____

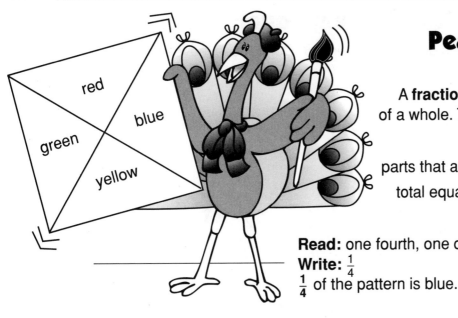

Peabo's Passion

A **fraction** is a number that names part of a whole. The whole represents 1.

parts that are blue→ **1** ← numerator

total equal parts→ **4** ← denominator

Read: one fourth, one out of four, or one divided by four

Write: $\frac{1}{4}$

$\frac{1}{4}$ of the pattern is blue.

Directions: For items 1–8, color each shape. Then write a fraction to complete the statement. For items 9 and 10, color each shape to match the statements. For items 11 and 12, divide and then color each shape to match the statements.

(color code: r = red, b = blue, g = green, y = yellow, o = orange, br = brown)

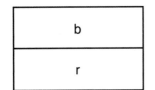

1. _____ is red.

2. _____ is yellow.

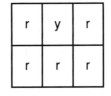

3. _____ is not red.

4. _____ is colored.

5. _____ is green.

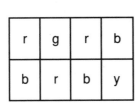

6. _____ is not red.

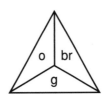

7. _____ is yellow.

8. _____ is green or red.

9. $\frac{2}{5}$ is yellow.
$\frac{1}{5}$ is blue.
$\frac{2}{5}$ is green.

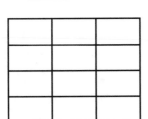

10. $\frac{7}{12}$ is brown.
$\frac{1}{12}$ is orange.
$\frac{4}{12}$ is green.

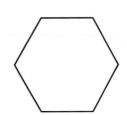

11. $\frac{1}{6}$ is red.
$\frac{5}{6}$ is blue.

12. $\frac{3}{10}$ is orange.
$\frac{3}{10}$ is blue.
$\frac{3}{10}$ is green.
$\frac{1}{10}$ is red.

"Leaf" Them Equal

Find the two equivalent fractions on each leaf cluster. Color those leaves green.

"Leaf" Them Equal

Find the two equivalent fractions on each leaf cluster. Color those leaves green.

Joking Around With Peabo

To find the answer to the riddle, write the decimals to complete each number line. Then write the matching letter in each box.

U = 0.56	R = 0.59	O = 0.54
F = 0.14	D = 0.8	A = 0.4
L = 0.7	Y = 0.52	O = 0.12
E = 0.5	A = 0.6	K = 0.9
T = 0.2	F = 0.17	H = 0.1

What do you get when you cross a parrot with a shark?
A bird that will...

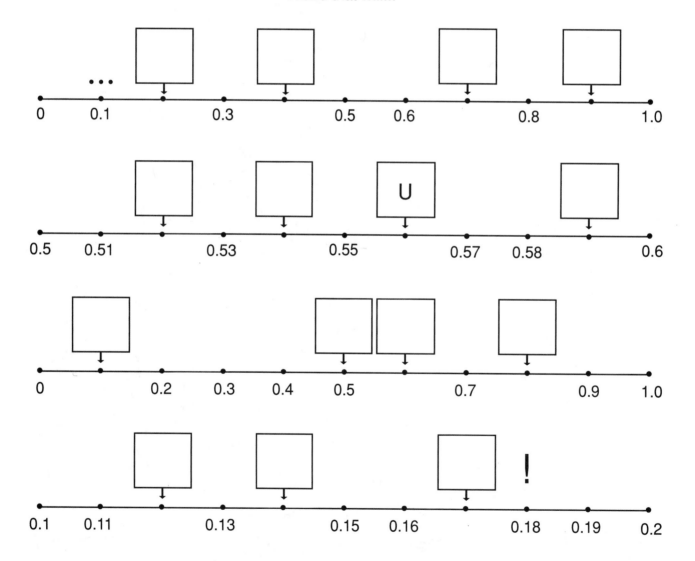

Joking Around With Peabo

To find the answer to the riddle, write the decimals to complete each number line. Then write the matching letter in each box.

U = 0.56	R = 0.59	O = 0.54
F = 0.14	D = 0.8	A = 0.4
L = 0.7	Y = 0.52	O = 0.12
E = 0.5	A = 0.6	K = 0.9
T = 0.2	F = 0.17	H = 0.1

What do you get when you cross a parrot with a shark?
A bird that will...

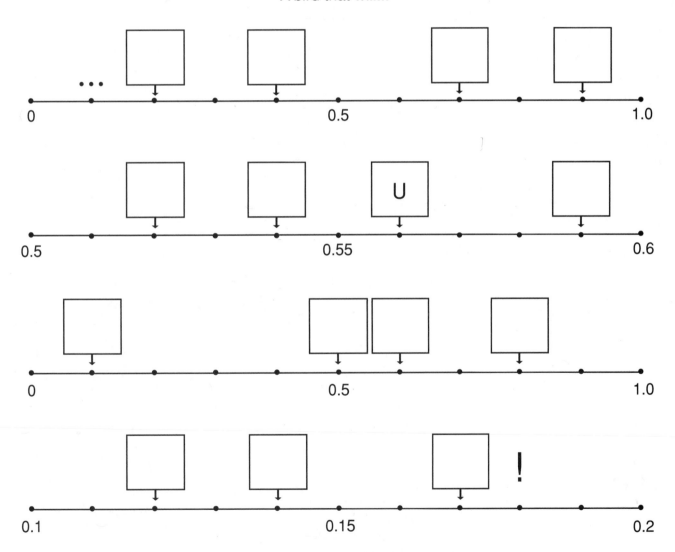

On a Journey for Jewels

Color if correct.

$\frac{4}{5} - \frac{2}{5} = \frac{2}{5}$

$\frac{1}{3} + \frac{1}{3} = \frac{2}{3}$

$\frac{2}{5} + \frac{2}{5} = \frac{4}{10}$

$\frac{7}{8} - \frac{2}{8} = \frac{5}{8}$

$\frac{1}{3} + \frac{1}{3} = \frac{2}{6}$

$\frac{2}{8} + \frac{2}{8} = \frac{4}{8}$

$\frac{5}{6} - \frac{1}{6} = \frac{4}{0}$

$\frac{2}{7} + \frac{3}{7} = \frac{5}{14}$

$\frac{2}{4} + \frac{1}{4} = \frac{3}{4}$

$\frac{3}{10} + \frac{3}{10} = \frac{6}{10}$

$\frac{6}{12} + \frac{1}{12} = \frac{7}{24}$

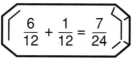

$\frac{5}{10} - \frac{3}{10} = \frac{2}{10}$

On a Journey for Jewels

Color if correct.

$\dfrac{1}{3} + \dfrac{1}{3} = \dfrac{2}{3}$

$\dfrac{3}{7} + \dfrac{2}{7} = \dfrac{5}{7}$

$\dfrac{2}{5} + \dfrac{2}{5} = \dfrac{4}{10}$

$\dfrac{1}{3} + \dfrac{1}{3} = \dfrac{2}{6}$

$\dfrac{4}{5} - \dfrac{2}{5} = \dfrac{2}{5}$

$\dfrac{1}{2} - \dfrac{1}{2} = 0$

$\dfrac{2}{7} + \dfrac{3}{7} = \dfrac{5}{14}$

$\dfrac{3}{10} + \dfrac{2}{10} = \dfrac{5}{20}$

$\dfrac{2}{8} + \dfrac{2}{8} = \dfrac{4}{8}$

$\dfrac{5}{9} - \dfrac{2}{9} = \dfrac{3}{9}$

$\dfrac{7}{8} - \dfrac{2}{8} = \dfrac{5}{8}$

$\dfrac{3}{10} + \dfrac{3}{10} = \dfrac{6}{10}$

$\dfrac{5}{6} - \dfrac{1}{6} = \dfrac{4}{0}$

$\dfrac{2}{4} + \dfrac{1}{4} = \dfrac{3}{4}$

$\dfrac{6}{12} + \dfrac{1}{12} = \dfrac{7}{24}$

$\dfrac{5}{10} - \dfrac{3}{10} = \dfrac{2}{10}$

$\dfrac{6}{9} - \dfrac{2}{9} = \dfrac{4}{18}$

Fraction Jewels

Solve each equation. Write each answer in simplest form.

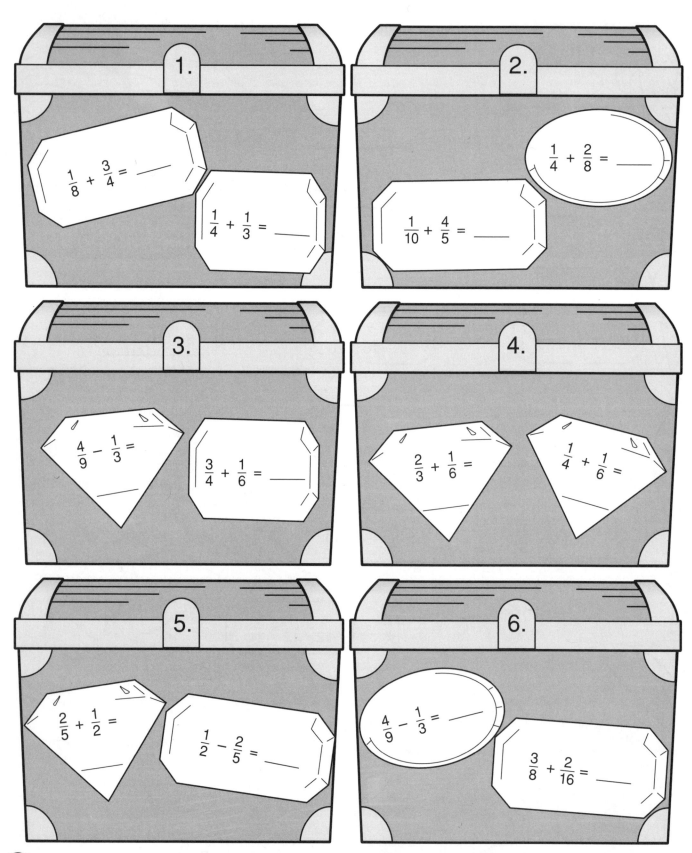

1.
$\frac{1}{8} + \frac{3}{4} = $ _____

$\frac{1}{4} + \frac{1}{3} = $ _____

2.
$\frac{1}{4} + \frac{2}{8} = $ _____

$\frac{1}{10} + \frac{4}{5} = $ _____

3.
$\frac{4}{9} - \frac{1}{3} = $ _____

$\frac{3}{4} + \frac{1}{6} = $ _____

4.
$\frac{2}{3} + \frac{1}{6} = $ _____

$\frac{1}{4} + \frac{1}{6} = $ _____

5.
$\frac{2}{5} + \frac{1}{2} = $ _____

$\frac{1}{2} - \frac{2}{5} = $ _____

6.
$\frac{4}{9} - \frac{1}{3} = $ _____

$\frac{3}{8} + \frac{2}{16} = $ _____

Fraction Jewels

Solve each equation. Write each answer in simplest form. Two of the answers will be the same. Mark an X through the answer that is different.

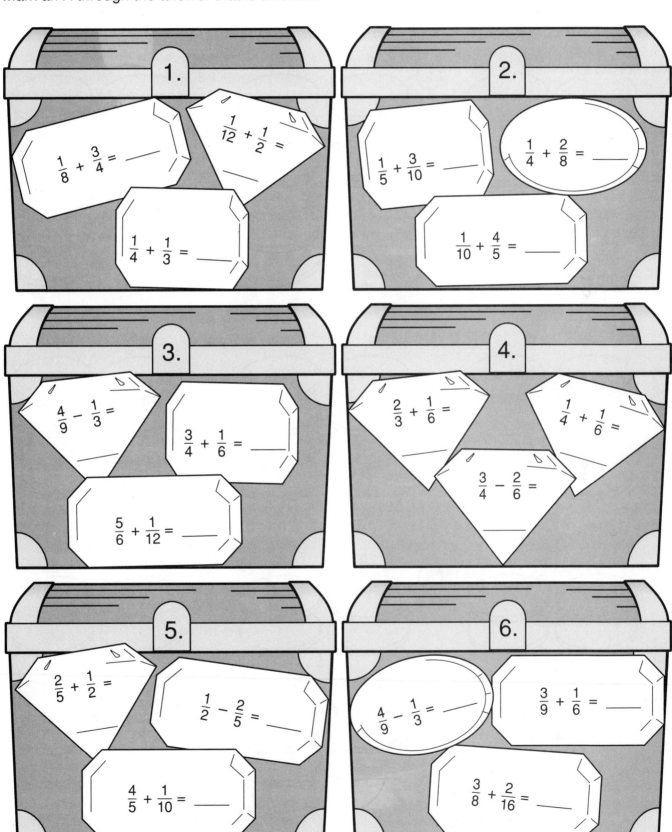

1.
$\frac{1}{8} + \frac{3}{4} =$ ___

$\frac{1}{12} + \frac{1}{2} =$ ___

$\frac{1}{4} + \frac{1}{3} =$ ___

2.
$\frac{1}{5} + \frac{3}{10} =$ ___

$\frac{1}{4} + \frac{2}{8} =$ ___

$\frac{1}{10} + \frac{4}{5} =$ ___

3.
$\frac{4}{9} - \frac{1}{3} =$ ___

$\frac{3}{4} + \frac{1}{6} =$ ___

$\frac{5}{6} + \frac{1}{12} =$ ___

4.
$\frac{2}{3} + \frac{1}{6} =$ ___

$\frac{1}{4} + \frac{1}{6} =$ ___

$\frac{3}{4} - \frac{2}{6} =$ ___

5.
$\frac{2}{5} + \frac{1}{2} =$ ___

$\frac{1}{2} - \frac{2}{5} =$ ___

$\frac{4}{5} + \frac{1}{10} =$ ___

6.
$\frac{4}{9} - \frac{1}{3} =$ ___

$\frac{3}{9} + \frac{1}{6} =$ ___

$\frac{3}{8} + \frac{2}{16} =$ ___

Name _____

Common Factor Coins

List the factors of each number below on the coins. Then write the greatest common factor of each pair of numbers on the line provided. The first one has been done for you.

1   **12**   **15**

1 1
2 ③
③ 5
4 15
6 GCF:
12 3

2   **4**   **12**

GCF:
_____

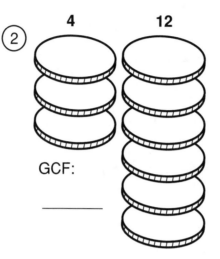

3   **9**   **18**

GCF:
_____

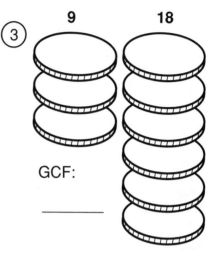

4   **10**   **25**

GCF: _____

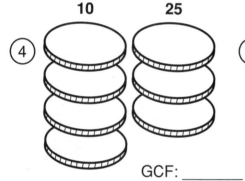

5   **4**   **14**

GCF: _____

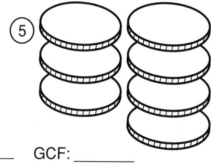

6   **21**   **27**

GCF: _____

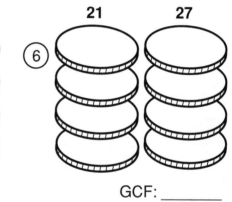

7   **28**   **35**

GCF:
_____

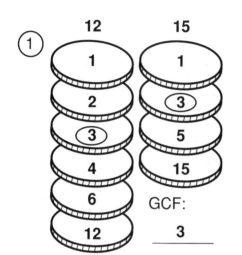

8   **20**   **30**

GCF:
_____

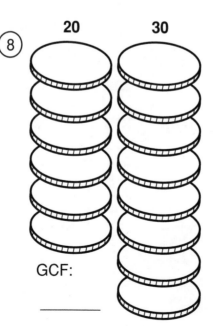

9   **8**   **12**

GCF:
_____

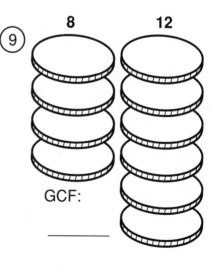

Name _____

Common Factor Coins

List the factors of each number below on the coins. Then write the greatest common factor of each pair of numbers on the line provided.

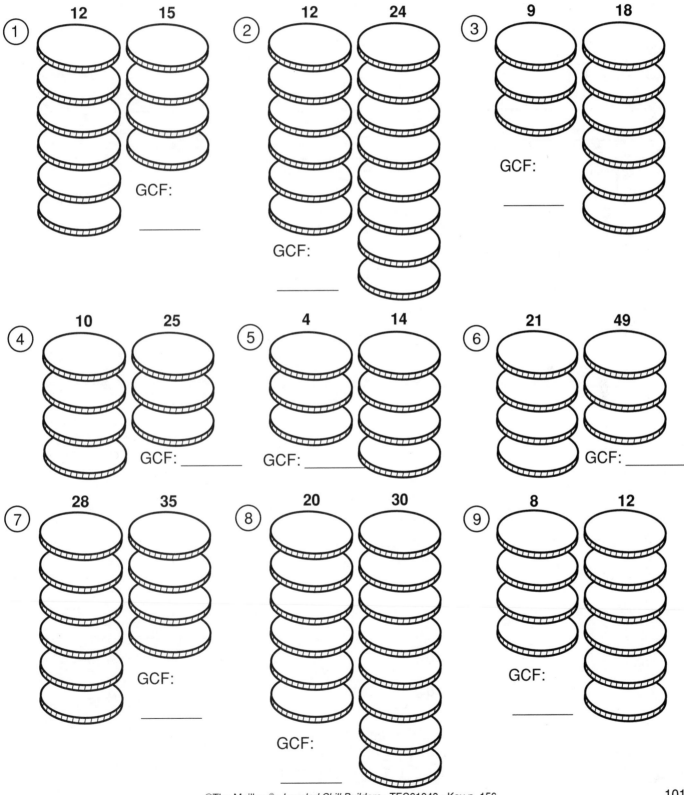

Treasure Trove

Solve each problem below. Write each answer in simplest form. Then write the letter on the matching blank.

Chest D: $7\frac{9}{10}$ $3\frac{3}{10}$ $4\frac{7}{10}$

Chest E: $3\frac{1}{3}$ $18\frac{7}{9}$ $10\frac{2}{3}$ $4\frac{2}{5}$ $1\frac{1}{8}$

Chest A / L: $15\frac{1}{3}$ $5\frac{2}{3}$ $1\frac{1}{3}$ $16\frac{5}{7}$

(R) $5\frac{7}{9}$
  $-2\frac{4}{9}$

(P) $8\frac{1}{6}$
  $+7\frac{1}{6}$

(O) $5\frac{6}{10}$
  $-2\frac{3}{10}$

(B) $3\frac{1}{6}$
  $+7\frac{3}{6}$

(I) $8\frac{3}{5}$
  $-4\frac{1}{5}$

(G) $5\frac{3}{10}$
  $+2\frac{6}{10}$

(S) $6\frac{3}{8}$
  $-5\frac{2}{8}$

(S) $9\frac{3}{7}$
  $+7\frac{2}{7}$

(E) $3\frac{1}{3}$
  $+2\frac{1}{3}$

(U) $10\frac{2}{9}$
  $+8\frac{5}{9}$

(R) $3\frac{2}{3}$
  $-2\frac{1}{3}$

(L) $9\frac{9}{10}$
  $-5\frac{2}{10}$

Name _____

Treasure Trove

Solve each problem below. Write each answer in simplest form. Then write the letter on the matching blank.

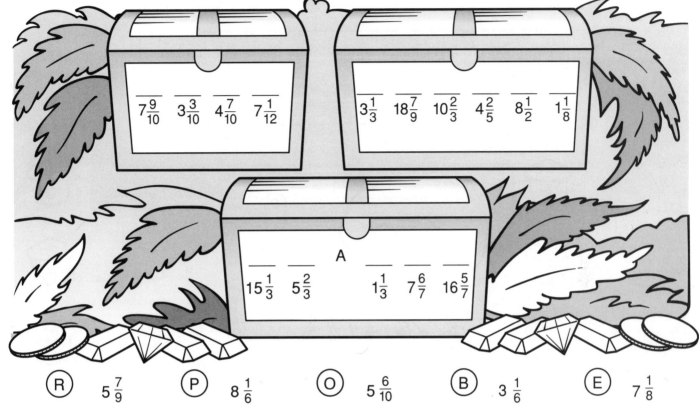

$$\overline{7\frac{9}{10}} \quad \overline{3\frac{3}{10}} \quad \overline{4\frac{7}{10}} \quad \overline{7\frac{1}{12}}$$

$$\overline{3\frac{1}{3}} \quad \overline{18\frac{7}{9}} \quad \overline{10\frac{2}{3}} \quad \overline{4\frac{2}{5}} \quad \overline{8\frac{1}{2}} \quad \overline{1\frac{1}{8}}$$

A

$$\overline{15\frac{1}{3}} \quad \overline{5\frac{2}{3}} \qquad \overline{1\frac{1}{3}} \quad \overline{7\frac{6}{7}} \quad \overline{16\frac{5}{7}}$$

(R) $\quad 5\frac{7}{9}$
$\quad -2\frac{4}{9}$

(P) $\quad 8\frac{1}{6}$
$\quad +7\frac{1}{6}$

(O) $\quad 5\frac{6}{10}$
$\quad -2\frac{3}{10}$

(B) $\quad 3\frac{1}{6}$
$\quad +7\frac{3}{6}$

(E) $\quad 7\frac{1}{8}$
$\quad +1\frac{3}{8}$

(I) $\quad 8\frac{3}{5}$
$\quad -4\frac{1}{5}$

(G) $\quad 5\frac{3}{10}$
$\quad +2\frac{6}{10}$

(S) $\quad 6\frac{3}{8}$
$\quad -5\frac{2}{8}$

(S) $\quad 9\frac{3}{7}$
$\quad +7\frac{2}{7}$

(D) $\quad 9\frac{9}{12}$
$\quad -2\frac{8}{12}$

(E) $\quad 3\frac{1}{3}$
$\quad +2\frac{1}{3}$

(U) $\quad 10\frac{2}{9}$
$\quad +8\frac{5}{9}$

(R) $\quad 3\frac{2}{3}$
$\quad -2\frac{1}{3}$

(L) $\quad 9\frac{9}{10}$
$\quad -5\frac{2}{10}$

(L) $\quad 3\frac{1}{7}$
$\quad +4\frac{5}{7}$

Name ———————————————————

Mixed-Up Message

Change each mixed number to an improper fraction. Then match the letters with the answers at the bottom of the page to solve the riddle on the note.

> Remember: Multiply the denominator by the whole number. Then add the numerator.
>
> $$1\frac{1}{3} = \frac{(1 \times 3) + 1}{3} = \frac{4}{3}$$

1. $2\frac{3}{5}$ = _____ A

2. $1\frac{1}{12}$ = _____ T

3. $3\frac{2}{3}$ = _____ F

4. $3\frac{1}{3}$ = _____ G

5. $5\frac{1}{4}$ = _____ O

6. $1\frac{5}{6}$ = _____ N

7. $7\frac{1}{2}$ = _____ U

8. $3\frac{1}{6}$ = _____ P

9. $4\frac{3}{4}$ = _____ H

10. $5\frac{2}{5}$ = _____ U

11. $1\frac{1}{2}$ = _____ D

12. $7\frac{2}{3}$ = _____ L

Good morning, Candy! Let's see whether you can solve my riddle before I get to the bakery. What has no beginning, no end, and nothing in the middle?

Good luck!
E. Clair

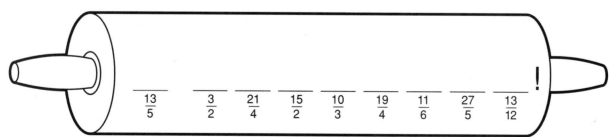

$$\frac{13}{5} \qquad \frac{3}{2} \qquad \frac{21}{4} \qquad \frac{15}{2} \qquad \frac{10}{3} \qquad \frac{19}{4} \qquad \frac{11}{6} \qquad \frac{27}{5} \qquad \frac{13}{12} \qquad !$$

Mixed-Up Message

Change each mixed number to an improper fraction. Then match the letters with the answers at the bottom of the page to solve the riddle on the note.

> Remember: Multiply the denominator by the whole number. Then add the numerator.
>
> $$1\frac{1}{3} = \frac{(1 \times 3) + 1}{3} = \frac{4}{3}$$

1. $2\frac{1}{2}$ = _____ **M**

2. $2\frac{3}{5}$ = _____ **A**

3. $1\frac{1}{12}$ = _____ **T**

4. $3\frac{2}{3}$ = _____ **F**

5. $3\frac{1}{3}$ = _____ **G**

6. $5\frac{1}{4}$ = _____ **O**

7. $6\frac{1}{8}$ = _____ **C**

8. $1\frac{5}{6}$ = _____ **N**

9. $9\frac{7}{8}$ = _____ **K**

10. $7\frac{1}{2}$ = _____ **U**

11. $3\frac{1}{6}$ = _____ **P**

12. $4\frac{3}{4}$ = _____ **H**

13. $4\frac{1}{10}$ = _____ **I**

14. $5\frac{2}{5}$ = _____ **U**

15. $1\frac{1}{2}$ = _____ **D**

16. $7\frac{2}{3}$ = _____ **L**

Good morning, Candy! Let's see whether you can solve my riddle before I get to the bakery. What has no beginning, no end, and nothing in the middle?

Good luck!
E. Clair

$\frac{13}{5}$ $\quad$ $\frac{3}{2}$ $\quad$ $\frac{21}{4}$ $\quad$ $\frac{15}{2}$ $\quad$ $\frac{10}{3}$ $\quad$ $\frac{19}{4}$ $\quad$ $\frac{11}{6}$ $\quad$ $\frac{27}{5}$ $\quad$ $\frac{13}{12}$ $\quad$!

Order Up!

Work backward to solve the problems below.

ORDER NO. 3464   SERVER NO. **6**

1. Danny started making food early for the lunch crowd. He chopped vegetables for 25 minutes and made salads for 20 minutes. He cooked soup and made the daily special for 50 minutes. Then he baked a cake and two pies. This took 1 hour and 5 minutes. If Danny stopped at 11:00 A.M., what time did he begin?

    _____

2. Danny baked a chocolate cake for dessert. The cake was cut into slices. Eight diners ordered cake for dessert at lunch. Half that many came in during the afternoon and ordered a slice. Danny and Wanda each had a slice for a snack. If 4 slices were left at the end of the day, how many slices were originally cut from the cake?

    _____

3. Customer Cal is one of Danny's regulars. He ate at the diner on Wednesday. He ordered the daily special, macaroni and cheese, for $2.95. He also ordered a milk shake that cost $1.25 and a piece of pie that cost $0.95. Cal left the diner with $18.53 in his wallet. How much money did he have when he entered the diner?

    _____

Order Up!

Work backward to solve the problems below.

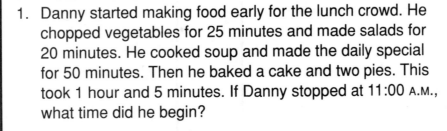

ORDER NO. 3464   SERVER NO. **6**

1. Danny started making food early for the lunch crowd. He chopped vegetables for 25 minutes and made salads for 20 minutes. He cooked soup and made the daily special for 50 minutes. Then he baked a cake and two pies. This took 1 hour and 5 minutes. If Danny stopped at 11:00 A.M., what time did he begin?

_____

2. Wanda the waitress took a break at 3 P.M. Before that she waited on tables for $2\frac{1}{2}$ hours. She also helped Danny make salads for 40 minutes. If it takes Wanda 35 minutes to travel from her house to Danny's Diner, what time did she leave her house to come to work?

_____

3. Danny's Diner served 17 customers during lunch. There were twice that many customers during dinner. The number of customers in the diner at the dinner hour was 7 fewer than the number of customers during breakfast. How many customers were in the diner during breakfast?

_____

4. Danny baked a chocolate cake for dessert. The cake was cut into slices. Eight diners ordered cake for dessert at lunch. Half that many came in during the afternoon and ordered a slice. Danny and Wanda each had a slice for a snack. If 4 slices were left at the end of the day, how many slices were originally cut from the cake?

_____

5. Customer Cal is one of Danny's regulars. He ate at the diner on Wednesday. He ordered the daily special, macaroni and cheese, for $2.95. He also ordered a milk shake that cost $1.25 and a piece of pie that cost $0.95. Cal left the diner with $18.53 in his wallet. How much money did he have when he entered the diner?

_____

Sir Siegfried's Feast

Use the guess-and-check strategy to solve each problem.

1. Minstrels, jugglers, and jesters provided entertainment at the feast. There were 3 more minstrels than jugglers, and twice as many jesters as jugglers. If the total number of entertainers was 11, how many were there of each entertainer?

   _____

   _____

2. For this feast, 142 different dishes of vegetables and fruits were prepared. If 42 more vegetable dishes were prepared than fruit dishes, how many dishes of each kind were served at the feast?

   _____

   _____

3. Altogether 178 people attended the feast. There were 44 more men than women who came. How many men and how many women attended the celebration?

   _____

   _____

©The Mailbox® • Leveled Skill Builders • TEC61040 • Key p. 157

Sir Siegfried's Feast

Use the guess-and-check strategy to solve each problem.

1. Minstrels, jugglers, and jesters provided entertainment at the feast. There were 3 more minstrels than jugglers, and twice as many jesters as jugglers. If the total number of entertainers was 11, how many were there of each entertainer?

   _____

   _____

2. For this feast, 142 different dishes of vegetables and fruits were prepared. If 42 more vegetable dishes were prepared than fruit dishes, how many dishes of each kind were served at the feast?

   _____

   _____

3. Altogether 178 people attended the feast. There were 44 more men than women who came. How many men and how many women attended the celebration?

   _____

   _____

4. Invitations were sent one week before the big event. Replies started coming in the following Monday. On Tuesday, 2 more replies had been received than on Monday. On Wednesday, 11 more than one half the number of replies received on Monday were received. If a total of 53 invitations were received during the first 3 days of that week, how many replies were received on Monday?

   _____

   _____

Name _____

Danny's Diner Data

Use the make-a-table strategy to solve each problem.

1. Wanda sees that about every 15 minutes 7 customers order the daily special. At this rate, how many daily specials will Danny make in 60 minutes? How many will he make in 2 hours?

Minutes								
Specials								

Solution: _____

2. Wanda serves 13 orders in 20 minutes. At this pace, how many orders will she serve in an hour? How long will it take for her to serve 104 orders?

Minutes								
Orders								

Solution: _____

Solve the problem below by making a table in the space provided. Then write the solution on the line.

3. Customer Cal eats at Danny's Diner every day. Every fourth day he orders chili. Every third day he orders chocolate pie for dessert. If Cal eats at the diner for 2 weeks, how many days will he eat chili and chocolate pie at the same meal?

Solution: _____

Name _____

Danny's Diner Data

Use the make-a-table strategy to solve each problem.

1. Wanda sees that about every 15 minutes 7 customers order the daily special. At this rate, how many daily specials will Danny make in 60 minutes? How many will he make in 2 hours?

Minutes									
Specials									

Solution: _____

2. Wanda serves 13 orders in 20 minutes. At this pace, how many orders will she serve in an hour? How long will it take for her to serve 104 orders?

Minutes								
Orders								

Solution: _____

Solve each of the problems below by making a table in the space provided. Then write each solution on the line.

3. Customer Cal eats at Danny's Diner every day. Every fourth day he orders chili. Every third day he orders chocolate pie for dessert. If Cal eats at the diner for 2 weeks, how many days will he eat chili and chocolate pie at the same meal?

Solution: _____

4. Wanda sees that every second person who comes into the diner orders the special. She sees every third person order dessert. Every sixth person orders a soft drink. If Wanda takes 20 orders, how many people will order a special, dessert, and soft drink?

Solution: _____

Trading Bedrooms

Otto and Olive are redecorating each other's room. Help them by converting the units for each measurement below. A hint is in parentheses.

Customary Units

12 inches (in.) = 1 foot (ft.)   3 feet (ft.) = 1 yard (yd.)

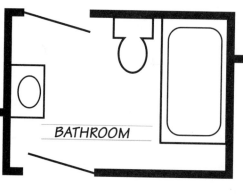

OLIVE'S ROOM

1. ladybug wallpaper border
   39 ft. = _____ yd. *(divide)*

2. length of green curtains
   132 in. = _____ ft. *(divide)*

3. length of purple curtain ties
   36 in. = _____ ft. *(divide)*

4. pink bookcase
   3 yd. = _____ ft. *(multiply)*

5. butterfly wall hanging
   96 in. = _____ ft. *(divide)*

6. height of pink nightstand
   4 ft. = _____ in. *(multiply)*

7. flower-shaped rug
   5 ft. x 8 ft. = _____ in. x _____ in.
   (multiply)

BATHROOM

OTTO'S ROOM

8. racecar wallpaper border
   8 yd. = _____ ft. *(multiply)*

9. red closet shelves
   12 ft. = _____ yd. *(divide)*

10. length of checkered flag curtains
    9 ft. = _____ in. *(multiply)*

11. width of car-shaped bed
    84 in. = _____ ft. *(divide)*

12. height of closet door
    8 ft. = _____ in. *(multiply)*

13. width of desk
    2 yd. = _____ ft. *(multiply)*

14. racetrack rug
    48 in. x 72 in. = _____ ft. x _____ ft.
    (divide)

Trading Bedrooms

Otto and Olive are redecorating each other's room. Help them by converting the units for each measurement below.

Customary Units
12 inches (in.) = 1 foot (ft.)   3 feet (ft.) = 1 yard (yd.)

OLIVE'S ROOM

1. ladybug wallpaper border
   39 ft. = _____ yd.

2. length of green curtains
   132 in. = _____ ft.

3. length of purple curtain ties
   36 in. = _____ ft.

4. pink bookcase
   3 yd. = _____ ft.

5. butterfly wall hanging
   96 in. = _____ ft.

6. height of pink nightstand
   4 ft. = _____ in.

7. flower-shaped rug
   5 ft. x 8 ft. = _____ in. x _____ in.

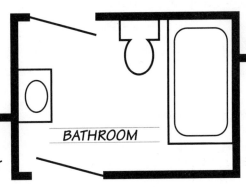

BATHROOM

OTTO'S ROOM

8. racecar wallpaper border
   8 yd. = _____ ft.

9. red closet shelves
   12 ft. = _____ yd.

10. length of checkered flag curtains
    9 ft. = _____ in.

11. width of car-shaped bed
    84 in. = _____ ft.

12. height of closet door
    8 ft. = _____ in.

13. width of desk
    2 yd. = _____ ft.

14. racetrack rug
    48 in. x 72 in. = _____ ft. x _____ ft.

Name _____

Read the clues below. Then draw a model of each shape in the space provided. Label each side of the drawing with its dimension. Two models have been done for you.

Perimeter: the distance around the outside of a closed figure
Area: the measure of the region inside a closed figure, measured in square units

1. a rectangle with a <u>perimeter</u> of 50 cm 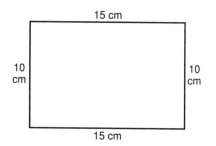	2. a regular hexagon with a <u>perimeter</u> of 36 in.	3. a square with an <u>area</u> of 144 square in.
4. a regular pentagon with a <u>perimeter</u> of 65 cm	5. a rectangle with an <u>area</u> of 50 square in.	6. a regular octagon with a <u>perimeter</u> of 64 cm
7. a trapezoid with a <u>perimeter</u> of 35 in. 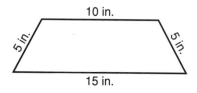	8. a square with a <u>perimeter</u> of 120 mm	9. a rectangle with a <u>length</u> of 60 mm and a <u>perimeter</u> of 200 mm

Name _____

Read the clues below. Then draw a model of each shape in the space provided. Label each side of the drawing with its dimension. Two models have been done for you.

> **Perimeter:** the distance around the outside of a closed figure
> **Area:** the measure of the region inside a closed figure, measured in square units

1. a rectangle with a perimeter of 50 cm 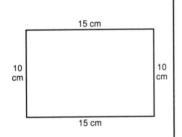	2. a regular hexagon with a perimeter of 36 in.	3. a square with an area of 144 square in.	4. a regular pentagon with a perimeter of 65 cm
5. an irregular 4-sided figure with a perimeter of 21 in.	6. a rectangle with an area of 50 square in.	7. a regular octagon with a perimeter of 64 cm	8. a trapezoid with a perimeter of 35 in. 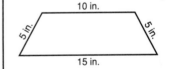
9. a square with a perimeter of 120 mm	10. a rectangle with a length of 60 mm and a perimeter of 200 mm	11. an irregular 7-sided figure with a perimeter of 121 cm	12. a parallelogram with a width of 52 mm and a perimeter of 180 mm

Container Calculations

Convert the unit of capacity on each bottle. Then color the bottle in each pair that shows the greater amount.

| 8 ounces (oz.) = 1 cup (c.) | 2 pints = 1 quart (qt.) |
| 2 cups = 1 pint (pt.) | 4 quarts = 1 gallon (gal.) |

Remember: Multiply to change from larger to smaller units. Divide to change from smaller to larger units.

1.

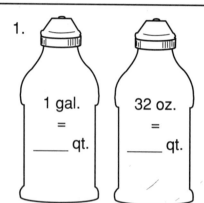

1 gal.
=
_____ qt.

32 oz.
=
_____ qt.

2.

16 oz.
=
_____ qt.

8 qt.
=
_____ gal.

3.

8 c.
=
_____ pt.

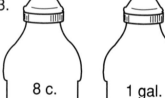

1 gal.
=
_____ c.

4.

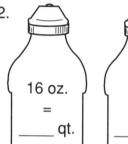

2 gal.
=
_____ qt.

6 pt.
=
_____ qt.

5.

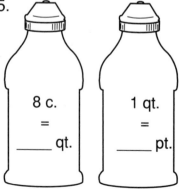

8 c.
=
_____ qt.

1 qt.
=
_____ pt.

6.

2 gal.
=
_____ oz.

3 pt.
=
_____ oz.

Name _____

Container Calculations

Convert the unit of capacity on each bottle. Then color the bottle in each pair that shows the greater amount.

8 ounces (oz.) = 1 cup (c.)	2 pints = 1 quart (qt.)
2 cups = 1 pint (pt.)	4 quarts = 1 gallon (gal.)

Remember: Multiply to change from larger to smaller units. Divide to change from smaller to larger units.

1.
1 gal.
=
____ qt.

32 oz.
=
____ qt.

2.
9 qt.
=
____ c.

32 c.
=
____ gal.

3.
16 oz.
=
____ qt.

8 qt.
=
____ gal.

4.
20 c.
=
____ pt.

4 gal.
=
____ c.

5.
3 gal.
=
____ qt.

10 pt.
=
____ qt.

6.
8 c.
=
____ qt.

11 qt.
=
____ pt.

7.
2 gal.
=
____ oz.

13 pt.
=
____ oz.

8.
24 oz.
=
____ pt.

5 qt.
=
____ pt.

9.
64 oz.
=
____ pt.

9 pt.
=
____ c.

©The Mailbox® • *Leveled Skill Builders* • TEC61040 • Key p. 158   117

Movin' Toward Measurement Success

Solve each measurement problem below. Write your answer on the matching truck.

1. _____

2. _____

3. _____

4. _____

1. On the way to one of his deliveries, T. Rucker's load weighs in at 7,500 pounds. Coming back, the load weighs in at 2 tons. How much of his load did he deliver? (Hint: 1 ton = 2,000 pounds)

2. If T. Rucker drinks enough soda to fill 20 cups, how many quarts of soda is this? (Hint: 4 cups = 1 quart)

3. T. Rucker begins cleaning his truck at 6:00 A.M. He finishes at 1:00 P.M. He takes an hour-long lunch. What is the total time he spends cleaning?

4. Should the temperature of T. Rucker's coffee be greater than or less than 40°F?

5. T. Rucker picks up three loads of trash to deliver to the recycling center. The first load weighs 756 pounds, the second 698 pounds, and the third 847 pounds. The trash can be compacted into half-ton loads. How many full half-ton loads can be made? How much will be left over? (Hint: 1 ton = 2,000 pounds)

6. On a delivery last month, T. Rucker began his return trip at 6:00 P.M. on Friday night. Anxious to get home, he kept driving for 2 days and 7 hours before he stopped. What day and time did he arrive home?

7. T. Rucker buys a six-pack of 12-ounce cans of soda. His friend buys a half-gallon of soda. Who buys more soda? (Hint: 1 gallon = 64 ounces)

8. The average person spends about 8 hours out of every 24 hours asleep. If T. Rucker is 30 years old, about how many years has he slept? (Hint: 1 year = 365 days)

5. _____

6. _____

7. _____

8. _____

Name_____

Movin' Toward Measurement Success

Solve each measurement problem below. Write your answer on the matching truck.

1. _____

2. _____

3. _____

4. _____

5. _____

1. On the way to one of his deliveries, T. Rucker's load weighs in at 7,500 pounds. Coming back, the load weighs in at 2 tons. How much of his load did he deliver?

2. Should the temperature in T. Rucker's truck cab be 55°F, 72°F, or 90°F?

3. If T. Rucker drinks enough soda to fill 20 cups, how many quarts of soda is this?

4. T. Rucker begins cleaning his truck at 6:00 A.M. He finishes at 1:00 P.M. He takes an hour-long lunch, a 20-minute break, and a 15-minute break. What is the total time he spends cleaning?

5. Should the temperature of T. Rucker's coffee be greater than or less than 40°F?

6. T. Rucker picks up three loads of trash to deliver to the recycling center. The first load weighs 756 pounds, the second 698 pounds, and the third 847 pounds. The trash can be compacted into half-ton loads. How many full half-ton loads can be made? How much will be left over?

7. On a delivery last month, T. Rucker began his return trip at 6:00 P.M. on Friday night. Anxious to get home, he kept driving for 2 days and 7 hours before he stopped. What day and time did he arrive home?

8. T. Rucker's pickup truck gets 32 miles to a gallon of gasoline. About how many fluid ounces of gasoline does the truck use to drive 1 mile?

9. T. Rucker buys a six-pack of 12-ounce cans of soda. His friend buys a half-gallon of soda. Who buys more soda?

10. The average person spends about 8 hours out of every 24 hours asleep. If T. Rucker is 30 years old, about how many years has he slept?

6. _____

7. _____

8. _____

9. _____

10. _____

Name _____

Bo and Bebe's Baby-Sitting

Complete the chart by filling in the missing information in each line. The first line has been done for you.

Reminder
To find the elapsed time between two times:
1. Count the hours from the first time to get as close as you can to the second time.
2. Then count the minutes to get to the second time.

Date	Beginning Time	Ending Time	Total Time Worked
1. Mon., Nov. 12	6:15 P.M.	8:30 P.M.	2 hrs. 15 mins.
2. Fri., Nov. 16	5:30 P.M.	10:20 P.M.	
3. Sat., Nov. 17	7:15 P.M.	11:50 P.M.	
4. Wed., Nov. 21	5:30 P.M.	9:20 P.M.	
5. Fri., Nov. 23	6:45 P.M.	10:20 P.M.	
6. Sat., Nov. 24	10:15 A.M.	4:00 P.M.	
7. Mon., Nov. 26	7:30 P.M.	9:45 P.M.	
8. Fri., Nov. 30	3:15 P.M.	10:40 P.M.	
9. Sat., Dec. 1		2:35 P.M.	4 hrs. 15 mins.
10. Thurs., Dec. 6	5:50 P.M.	8:40 P.M.	
11. Fri., Dec. 7		12:15 A.M.	6 hrs. 25 mins.
12. Sat., Dec. 8	11:45 A.M.		5 hrs. 30 mins.

Solve the following problem.

13. Bo got home from school at 4:15 P.M.
On the way home, he spent 30 minutes at the library and 15 minutes at the drugstore. It took Bo 20 minutes to walk home. At what time did Bo leave school?

_____

Name_____

Bo and Bebe's Baby-Sitting

Complete the chart by filling in the missing information in each line. The first line has been done for you.

Reminder

To find the elapsed time between two times:

1. Count the hours from the first time to get as close as you can to the second time.
2. Then count the minutes to get to the second time.

Date	Beginning Time	Ending Time	Total Time Worked
1. Mon., Nov. 12	6:15 P.M.	8:30 P.M.	2 hrs. 15 mins.
2. Fri., Nov. 16	5:30 P.M.	10:20 P.M.	
3. Sat., Nov. 17	7:15 P.M.		4 hrs. 35 mins.
4. Wed., Nov. 21		9:20 P.M.	3 hrs. 50 mins.
5. Fri., Nov. 23	6:45 P.M.		3 hrs. 35 mins.
6. Sat., Nov. 24	10:15 A.M.	4:00 P.M.	
7. Mon., Nov. 26	7:30 P.M.	9:45 P.M.	
8. Fri., Nov. 30	3:15 P.M.		7 hrs. 25 mins.
9. Sat., Dec. 1		2:35 P.M.	4 hrs. 15 mins.
10. Thurs., Dec. 6	5:50 P.M.	8:40 P.M.	
11. Fri., Dec. 7		12:15 A.M.	6 hrs. 25 mins.
12. Sat., Dec. 8	11:45 A.M.		5 hrs. 30 mins.

Solve the following problems.

13. Bo got home from school at 4:15 P.M. On the way home, he spent 30 minutes at the library and 15 minutes at the drugstore. It took Bo 20 minutes to walk home. At what time did Bo leave school?

_____

14. Bebe has to be at a baby-sitting job at 10:00 A.M. It takes her 35 minutes to shower and get dressed, 25 minutes to eat breakfast, and 15 minutes to walk to the job. At what time should she plan to get up?

_____

Window Planes

Graph the coordinates in each box. Connect the points, in order, to create the named plane figure. The first one is started for you.

Coordinates	Plane Figure
1. (0,3), (2,1), (4,1), (2,3)	parallelogram
2. (4,3), (4,2), (5,1), (6,1), (7,2), (7,3), (6,4), (5,4)	octagon
3. (7,0), (10,1), (9,3)	triangle
4. (12,2), (13,3), (14,3), (15,2)	trapezoid
5. (8,6), (7,5), (8,4), (9,4), (10,5), (9,6)	hexagon
6. (11,5), (11,9), (13,9), (13,5)	rectangle
7. (5,9), (3,8), (4,6), (6,6), (7,8)	pentagon

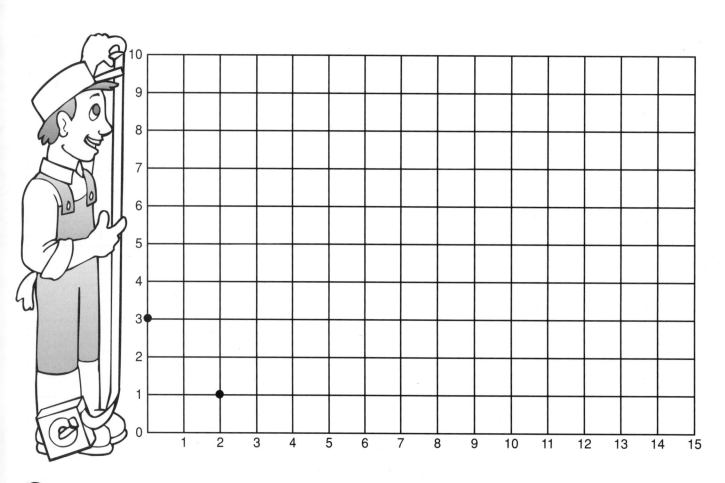

Name _____

Window Planes

Graph the coordinates in each box. Connect the points in order. Then write the name of each plane figure you create.

Coordinates	Plane Figure
1. (0,3), (2,1), (4,1), (2,3)	
2. (4,3), (4,2), (5,1), (6,1), (7,2), (7,3), (6,4), (5,4)	
3. (7,0), (10,1), (9,3)	
4. (12,2), (13,3), (14,3), (15,2)	
5. (8,6), (7,5), (8,4), (9,4), (10,5), (9,6)	
6. (11,5), (11,9), (13,9), (13,5)	
7. (5,9), (3,8), (4,6), (6,6), (7,8)	

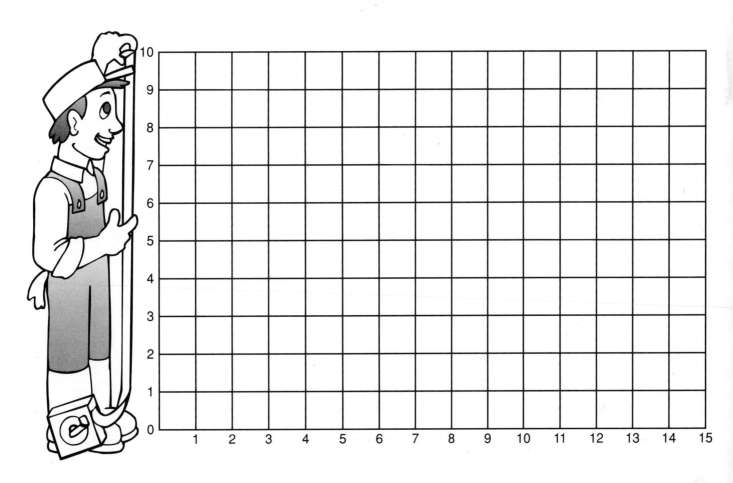

Name _____

Symmetry by Design

Decide whether each shape has line symmetry, point symmetry, both, or neither. Then color by the code.

A figure has *line symmetry* if it can be folded and unfolded so that the opposite sides are mirror reflections.

yes   **no**

A figure has *point symmetry* if it can be turned on a certain point so that it looks exactly the same in at least two different positions.

yes   **no**

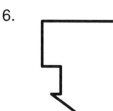

1.	2.	3.
4.	5. 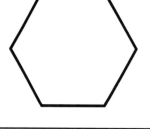	6.
7. 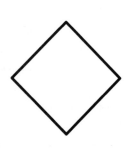	8. 	9. 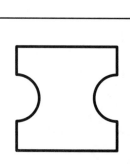

Name _____

Symmetry by Design

Decide whether each shape has line symmetry, point symmetry, both, or neither. Then color by the code.

A figure has *line symmetry* if it can be folded and unfolded so that the opposite sides are mirror reflections.

yes   **no**

A figure has *point symmetry* if it can be turned on a certain point so that it looks exactly the same in at least two different positions.

yes   **no**

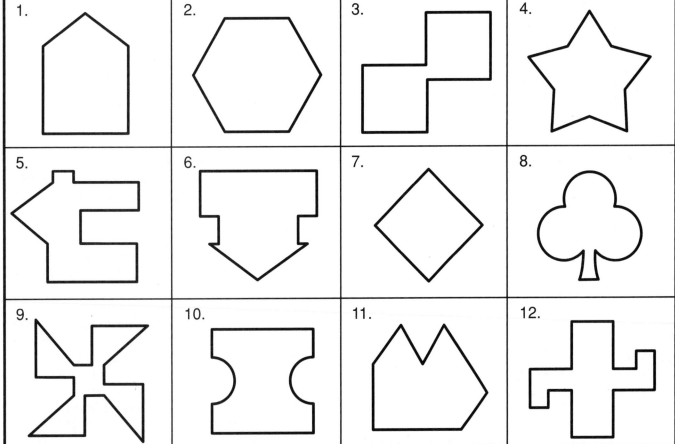

1.   2.   3.   4.

5.   6.   7.   8.

9.   10.   11.   12.

Lining the Route

Use the clues to label each missing location on the fairgrounds map. Then color the cotton candy symbol for each clue after you've completed it.

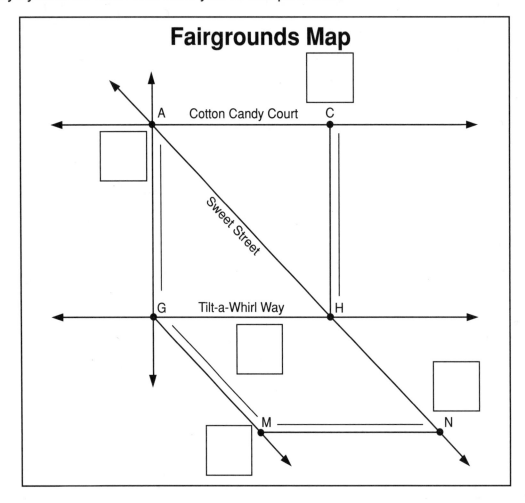

Fairgrounds Map

A — Cotton Candy Court — C

Sweet Street

G — Tilt-a-Whirl Way — H

M ————————— N

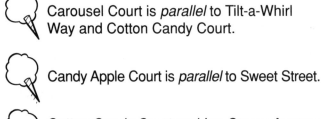
Carousel Court is *parallel* to Tilt-a-Whirl Way and Cotton Candy Court.

Candy Apple Court is *parallel* to Sweet Street.

Cotton Candy Court and Ice-Cream Avenue *intersect* at point C.

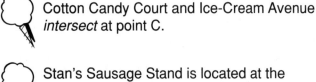
Stan's Sausage Stand is located at the *intersection* of Cotton Candy Court and Ice-Cream Avenue. Draw a ⌣ to show its location on the map.

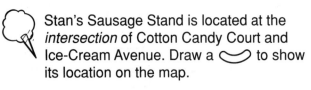
Ice-Cream Avenue and Ride Road are *perpendicular* to Tilt-a-Whirl Way.

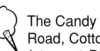
The Candy Barrel is located where Ride Road, Cotton Candy Court, and Sweet Street *intersect*. Draw a 🍭 to show its location on the map.

The Ferris wheel is on Sweet Street, along $\overrightarrow{HN}$. Draw a ⊕ to show its location on the map.

The roller coaster is between Tilt-a-Whirl Way and a road that runs *parallel* to it. Draw a 〰 to show its location on the map.

The carousel is located at point M on Candy Apple Court. Draw a ⌂ to show its location on the map.

Name _____

Lining the Route

Use the clues to label each missing location on the fairgrounds map. Then color the cotton candy symbol for each clue after you've completed it.

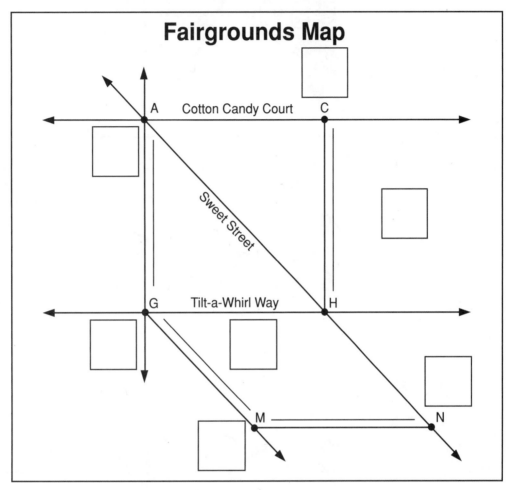

Fairgrounds Map

Cotton Candy Court

Sweet Street

Tilt-a-Whirl Way

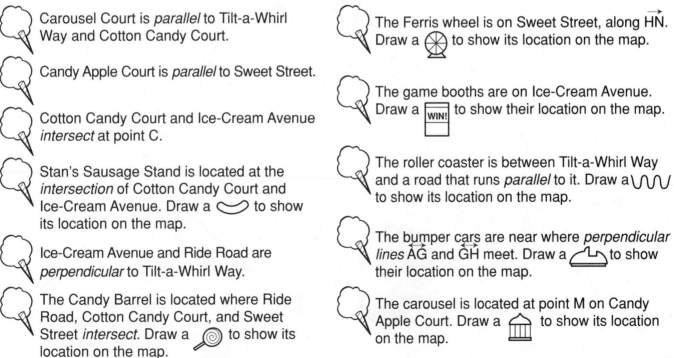

Carousel Court is *parallel* to Tilt-a-Whirl Way and Cotton Candy Court.

Candy Apple Court is *parallel* to Sweet Street.

Cotton Candy Court and Ice-Cream Avenue *intersect* at point C.

Stan's Sausage Stand is located at the *intersection* of Cotton Candy Court and Ice-Cream Avenue. Draw a ⌒ to show its location on the map.

Ice-Cream Avenue and Ride Road are *perpendicular* to Tilt-a-Whirl Way.

The Candy Barrel is located where Ride Road, Cotton Candy Court, and Sweet Street *intersect*. Draw a 🍭 to show its location on the map.

The Ferris wheel is on Sweet Street, along $\overrightarrow{HN}$. Draw a ⊕ to show its location on the map.

The game booths are on Ice-Cream Avenue. Draw a WIN! to show their location on the map.

The roller coaster is between Tilt-a-Whirl Way and a road that runs *parallel* to it. Draw a ⌇⌇⌇ to show its location on the map.

The bumper cars are near where *perpendicular* lines $\overleftrightarrow{AG}$ and $\overleftrightarrow{GH}$ meet. Draw a ⌂ to show their location on the map.

The carousel is located at point M on Candy Apple Court. Draw a 🎠 to show its location on the map.

Name _____

Acrobatic Angles

Write *acute*, *right*, or *obtuse* for each angle below.

> An *acute* angle measures less than 90°. A *right* angle measures exactly 90°. An *obtuse* angle measures more than 90° and less than 180°.

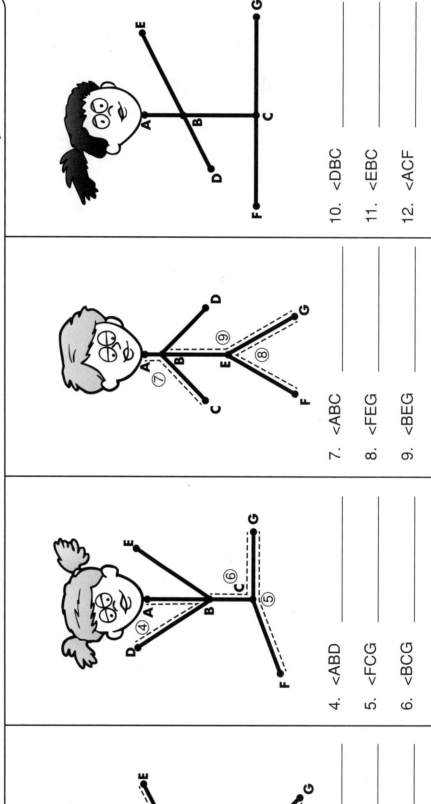

1. <ADE _____

2. <ADC _____

3. <BFG _____

4. <ABD _____

5. <FCG _____

6. <BCG _____

7. <ABC _____

8. <FEG _____

9. <BEG _____

10. <DBC _____

11. <EBC _____

12. <ACF _____

©The Mailbox® • *Leveled Skill Builders* • TEC61040 • Key p. 159

Name _____

Acrobatic Angles

Write *acute*, *right*, or *obtuse* for each angle below.

An *acute* angle measures less than 90°.   A *right* angle measures exactly 90°.   An *obtuse* angle measures more than 90° and less than 180°.

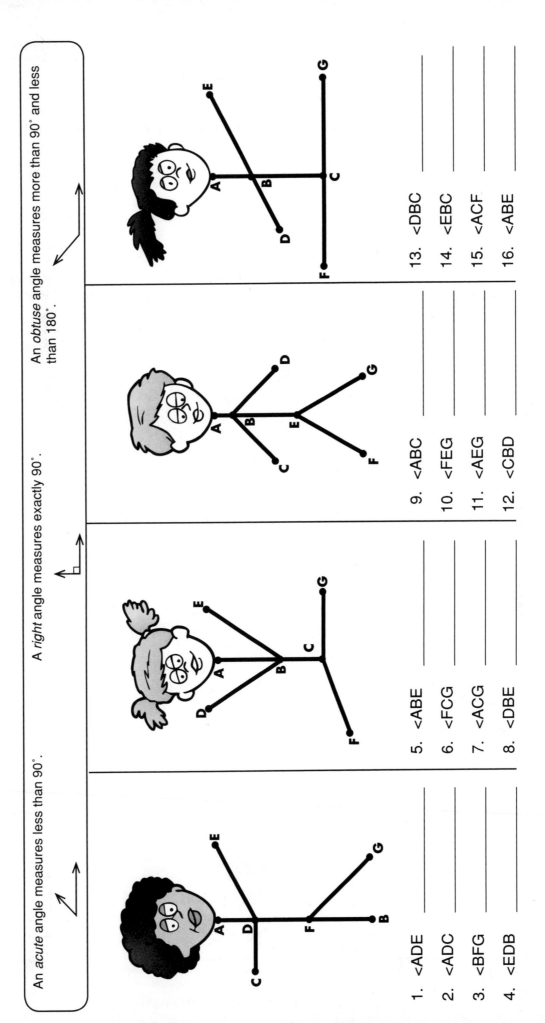

1. <ADE _____

2. <ADC _____

3. <BFG _____

4. <EDB _____

5. <ABE _____

6. <FCG _____

7. <ACG _____

8. <DBE _____

9. <ABC _____

10. <FEG _____

11. <AEG _____

12. <CBD _____

13. <DBC _____

14. <EBC _____

15. <ACF _____

16. <ABE _____

©The Mailbox® • *Leveled Skill Builders* • TEC61040 • Key p. 159

Name _____

It's on the Tag

Look at the figure on each tag. Fill in the number of faces, edges, and vertices.

1

Neil N. Hammer Building Company
Item: **Square Pyramid**

Number of edges: _8_

Number of vertices: _5_

Number of faces: _____

2

Neil N. Hammer Building Company
Item: **Cube**

Number of edges: _12_

Number of vertices: _____

Number of faces: _____

3

Neil N. Hammer Building Company
Item: **Triangular Pyramid**

Number of edges: _____

Number of vertices: _____

Number of faces: _4_

4

Neil N. Hammer Building Company
Item: **Rectangular Prism**

Number of edges: _____

Number of vertices: _8_

Number of faces: _____

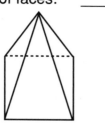
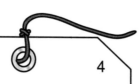
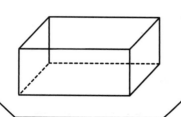

5

Neil N. Hammer Building Company
Item: **Sphere**

Number of edges: _____

Number of vertices: _____

Number of faces: _0_

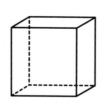

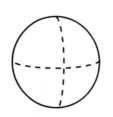

6

Neil N. Hammer Building Company
Item: **Triangular Prism**

Number of edges: _9_

Number of vertices: _____

Number of faces: _____

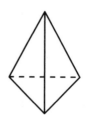

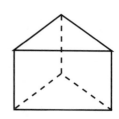

It's on the Tag

Look at the figure on each tag. Fill in the number of faces, edges, and vertices.

1

Neil N. Hammer Building Company

Item: **Square Pyramid**

Number of edges: _____

Number of vertices: _____

Number of faces: _____

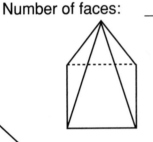

2

Neil N. Hammer Building Company

Item: **Cube**

Number of edges: _____

Number of vertices: _____

Number of faces: _____

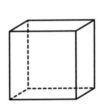

3

Neil N. Hammer Building Company

Item: **Triangular Pyramid**

Number of edges: _____

Number of vertices: _____

Number of faces: _____

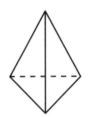

4

Neil N. Hammer Building Company

Item: **Rectangular Prism**

Number of edges: _____

Number of vertices: _____

Number of faces: _____

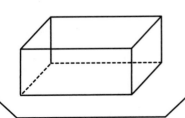

5

Neil N. Hammer Building Company

Item: **Sphere**

Number of edges: _____

Number of vertices: _____

Number of faces: _____

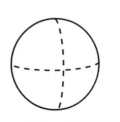

6

Neil N. Hammer Building Company

Item: **Triangular Prism**

Number of edges: _____

Number of vertices: _____

Number of faces: _____

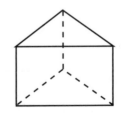

Tumbling Over Transformations

Translation or Slide	Reflection or Flip	Rotation or Turn
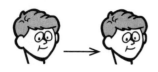		

Part 1: Label each move as a translation, reflection, or rotation.

Part 2: Cut out the boxes at the bottom of the page. Find the gymnast who shows the move indicated for each problem. Glue the cutout in place.

1. _____

2. _____

3. _____

4. _____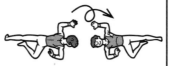

5. _____

1. rotation

2. reflection

3. translation

4. rotation

5. reflection

 a   b  c   d  e

Tumbling Over Transformations

Translation or Slide	**Reflection or Flip**	**Rotation or Turn**
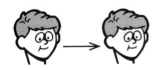		

Part 1: Label each move as a translation, reflection, or a rotation.

Part 2: Cut out the boxes at the bottom of the page. Find the gymnast who shows the move indicated for each problem. Glue the cutout in place.

1. _____

1. rotation

2. _____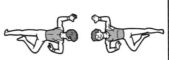

2. reflection

3. _____

3. translation

4. _____

4. rotation

5. _____

5. reflection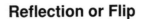

a	**b**	**c**	**d**	**e**

Name _____

Anna's New Games

Anna Log wants to create a new computer game called *Cool and Crazy Wheels.* She can feature cars, trucks, or motorcycles in the game. She can also include a spinner, dice, or number cards.

Part 1

1. The chart below shows all the possible choices for Anna's game. Read through it and fill in the blanks.

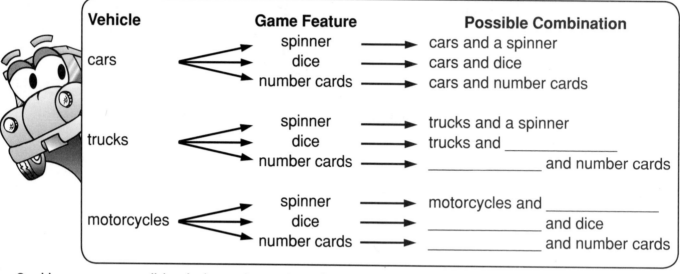

Vehicle	Game Feature	Possible Combination
cars	spinner	cars and a spinner
	dice	cars and dice
	number cards	cars and number cards
trucks	spinner	trucks and a spinner
	dice	trucks and _____
	number cards	_____ and number cards
motorcycles	spinner	motorcycles and _____
	dice	_____ and dice
	number cards	_____ and number cards

2. How many possible choices above does Anna have for her new game? _____

3. What is the probability that Anna will create a game about trucks and number cards?
   _____ out of _____, or $\frac{1}{9}$

4. What is the probability that Anna's game will include cars and a spinner?
   _____ out of _____, or _____

Part 2

Anna wants to create a game about space aliens and sports. She can include Martians, Plutonians, or Venusians. The sports she can choose from are baseball, tennis, and soccer. Fill in the chart to show all of Anna's possible choices.

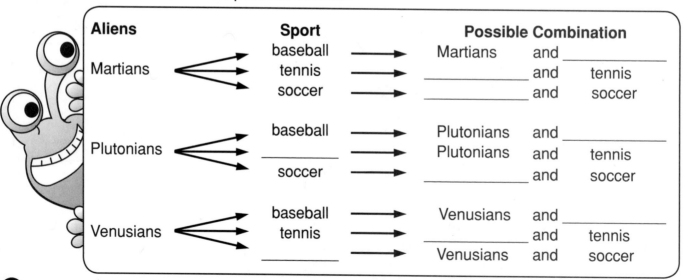

Aliens	Sport	Possible Combination
Martians	baseball	Martians and _____
	tennis	_____ and tennis
	soccer	_____ and soccer
Plutonians	baseball	Plutonians and _____
	_____	Plutonians and tennis
	soccer	_____ and soccer
Venusians	baseball	Venusians and _____
	tennis	_____ and tennis
	_____	Venusians and soccer

Name _____

Anna's New Games

Anna Log wants to create a new computer game called *Cool and Crazy Wheels.* She can feature cars, trucks, or motorcycles in the game. She can also include a spinner, dice, or number cards.

Part 1

1. The chart below shows all the possible choices for Anna's game. Read through it and fill in the blanks.

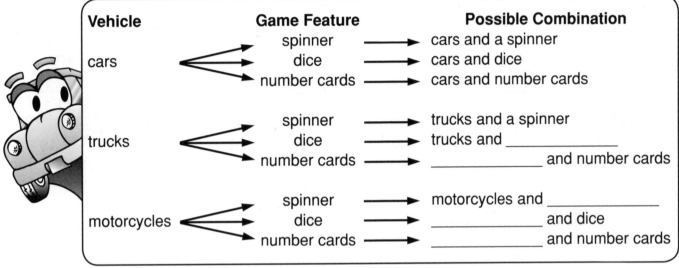

Vehicle	Game Feature	Possible Combination
cars	spinner	cars and a spinner
	dice	cars and dice
	number cards	cars and number cards
trucks	spinner	trucks and a spinner
	dice	trucks and _____
	number cards	_____ and number cards
motorcycles	spinner	motorcycles and _____
	dice	_____ and dice
	number cards	_____ and number cards

2. How many possible choices above does Anna have for her new game? _____

3. What is the probability that Anna will create a game about trucks and number cards?
   _____ out of _____, or $\frac{1}{9}$

4. What is the probability that Anna's game will include cars and a spinner?
   _____ out of _____, or _____

Part 2

Anna wants to create a game about space aliens and sports. She can include Martians, Plutonians, or Venusians. The sports she can choose from are baseball, tennis, and soccer. Fill in the chart to show all of Anna's possible choices.

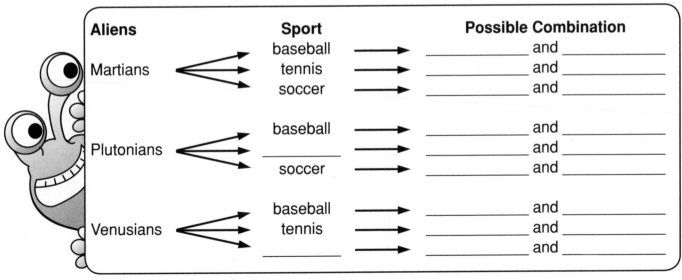

Aliens	Sport	Possible Combination
Martians	baseball	_____ and _____
	tennis	_____ and _____
	soccer	_____ and _____
Plutonians	baseball	_____ and _____
	_____	_____ and _____
	soccer	_____ and _____
Venusians	baseball	_____ and _____
	tennis	_____ and _____
	_____	_____ and _____

Surefire Statistics

A. The committee members of the Rocketown Fireworks Festival are comparing how much money each person collected during the weeklong event. Find the mean, median, mode, and range for each member's set of data. Write your answers in the chart. Then use the data to answer the questions that follow.

						Mean	Median	Mode	Range
Sparky X. Plode	$25	$27	$25	$31	$32				
Bea Lastoff	$42	$65	$29	$47	$42				
Iggie Nite	$38	$39	$38	$38	$32				
Flash N. Boom	$14	$30	$26	$14	$76				

1. Which person has the highest average? _____

2. Which person has the most money on any given day? _____
   How much? _____

3. Which two people have the widest range? _____

B. The stem-and-leaf graph shows the money collected by the committee members.
Use it to help you answer the questions at the right.

Stem	Leaves
1	4 4
2	5 5 6 7 9
3	0 1 2 2 8 8 8 9
4	2 2 7
5	
6	5
7	6

1. What is the median? _____
   _____

2. Which amount occurs most often (mode)? _____
   _____

3. What is the range of all the amounts collected?
   _____

Name _____

 **Surefire Statistics**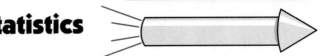

A. The committee members of the Rocketown Fireworks Festival are comparing how much money each person collected during the weeklong event. Find the mean, median, mode, and range for each member's set of data. Write your answers in the chart. Then use the data to answer the questions that follow.

								Mean	Median	Mode	Range
Sparky X. Plode	$25	$27	$26	$25	$31	$30	$25				
Bea Lastoff	$42	$48	$65	$29	$47	$42	$49				
Iggie Nite	$38	$39	$38	$40	$35	$32	$37				
Flash N. Boom	$14	$29	$21	$58	$26	$14	$76				

1. Which person has the highest average? _____

2. Which person has the most money on any given day? _____
   How much? _____

3. Which two people have the widest range? _____

4. If the festival continues one more day, about how much money can Iggie expect to collect:
   $28, $38, or $48? _____ Explain your answer. _____
   _____
   _____

B. Now use the data to complete a stem-and-leaf graph to show the money collected by the committee members. Then answer the questions at the right.

Stem	Leaves
1	
2	
3	
4	
5	
6	
7	

1. What is the mean of the data? _____
   _____

2. What is the median? _____
   _____

3. Which amount occurs most often (mode)? _____
   _____

4. What is the range of all the amounts collected?
   _____

Earth Agents to the Rescue!

One day each week, members of Cape View Elementary's Earth Agents Club collect trash around the school. Then they separate the items that can be recycled. Here is a graph showing how many items the club has collected for recycling in recent weeks.

Earth Agents Trash Collection

	Week 33	Week 34	Week 35	Week 36

cans ▨   bottles ☐

Part 1: Complete the graph using the following data.

- In week 35, Garrett, MacKenzie, and Sydney collected 19 cans and 7 bottles.
- In week 36, Brandon, Summer, Kameron, and Adrienne collected 3 cans and 1 bottle.

Part 2: Use the graph to answer the questions below.

1. In which week did the Earth Agents collect the most cans? _____ How many did they collect? _____

2. In which week did they collect the fewest bottles? _____ How many did they collect? _____

3. Which was collected more: cans or bottles? _____

4. Which is easier to read more quickly, the information as shown in Part 1 or the information as shown in the graph? _____ Explain your answer. _____

_____

_____

Name _____

Earth Agents to the Rescue!

One day each week, members of Cape View Elementary's Earth Agents Club collect trash around the school. Then they separate the items that can be recycled. Here is a graph showing how many items the club has collected for recycling in recent weeks.

Earth Agents Trash Collection

cans ☐   bottles ☐

Part 1: Complete the graph using the following data.
- In week 35, Garrett, MacKenzie, and Sydney collected 19 cans and 7 bottles.
- In week 36, Brandon, Summer, Kameron, and Adrienne collected 3 cans and 1 bottle.

Part 2: Use the graph to answer the questions below.

1. In which week did the Earth Agents collect the most cans? _____ How many did they collect? _____

2. In which week did they collect the fewest bottles? _____ How many did they collect? _____

3. Which was collected more: cans or bottles? _____

4. Which is easier to read more quickly, the information as shown in Part 1 or the information as shown in the graph? _____ Explain your answer. _____

   _____

   _____

5. The students sold some of the cans to a recycling center. With the money, they bought large garbage cans. They placed them near stop signs on each street around their school. When do you think the garbage cans were put in place? Use the data from the chart to support your answer. _____

   _____

   _____

Grade A Graphs

Study the graph below. Then answer the questions.

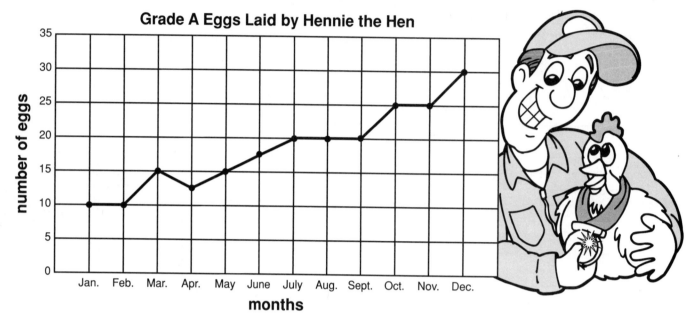

Grade A Eggs Laid by Hennie the Hen

months

1. How many eggs did Hennie lay in November? _____

2. How many more eggs did Hennie lay in August than in January? _____

3. For three months in a row, Hennie laid the same number of eggs. How many eggs did she lay each month? _____

4. During which months did she lay fewer than 15 eggs? _____

_____

Create your own line graph to show the number of eggs laid by Hennie's two sisters, Feathers and Chickie.

Use a blue colored pencil to track Feathers's eggs and a red one to track Chickie's eggs.

Year	Chickie	Feathers
2002	100	175
2001	150	125
2000	100	200
1999	225	100
1998	200	100
1997	175	125

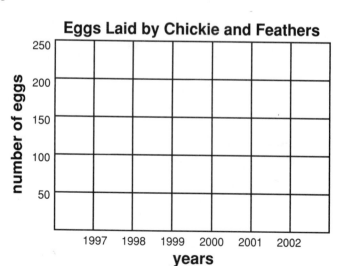

Eggs Laid by Chickie and Feathers

number of eggs

years

Name _____

Grade A Graphs

Study the graph below. Then answer the questions.

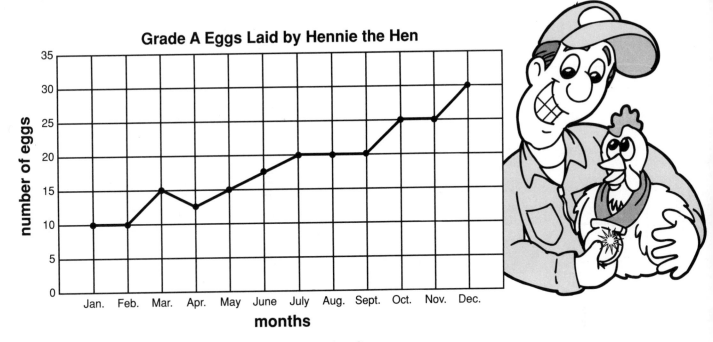

1. How many eggs did Hennie lay in November? _____

2. How many more eggs did Hennie lay in August than in January? _____

3. For three months in a row, Hennie laid the same number of eggs. How many eggs did she lay each month? _____

4. During which months did she lay fewer than 15 eggs? _____

_____

Now create your own line graph to show the number of eggs laid by Hennie's two sisters, Feathers and Chickie. Follow the steps below.

A. Choose a reasonable scale. Remember that a *scale* is the series of numbers placed at fixed distances on the graph. A *reasonable scale* is one for which most data fall on the scale lines.

B. Use a blue colored pencil to track Feathers's eggs and a red one to track Chickie's eggs.

C. Label each axis and give your graph a title.

Year	Chickie	Feathers
2002	100	175
2001	150	125
2000	100	200
1999	225	100
1998	200	100
1997	175	125

Name _____

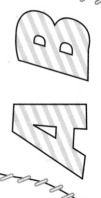

Piece by Piece

Write the letter that matches the rule for the pattern.
Then continue the pattern. A few have been started for you.

Rules

A. Alternate dividing by 3 with multiplying by 6.

B. Add 11, add 22, add 33, etc.

C. Add 9.

D. Add 7.

E. Alternate subtracting 15 with subtracting 10.

F. Alternate multiplying by 2 with adding 5.

G. Add 1, add 2, add 3, etc.

H. Multiply by 3.

I. Divide by 2.

J. Alternate subtracting 4 with adding 3.

[D] 1. 6, 13, 20, 27, 34 , ____, …

[ ] 2. 4, 12, 36, 108, ____, ____, …

[ ] 3. 30, 10, 60, 20, ____, ____, …

[E] 4. 100, 85, 75, 60, ____, ____, …

[B] 5. 11, 22, 44, 77, ____, ____, …

[ ] 6. 24, 20, 23, 19, 22, ____, ____, …

[ ] 7. 10, 19, 28, 37, 46, ____, ____, …

[ ] 8. 2, 3, 5, 8, 12, ____, ____, …

[F] 9. 3, 6, 11, ____, 27, 54, ____, …

[ ] 10. 96, ____, ____, 24, 12, ____, 3, …

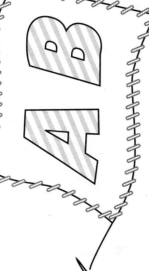

Piece by Piece

Write the letter that matches the rule for the pattern.
Then continue the pattern.

Rules

A. Alternate dividing by 3 with multiplying by 6.

B. Add 11, add 22, add 33, etc.

C. Add 9.

D. Add 7.

E. Alternate subtracting 15 with subtracting 10.

F. Alternate multiplying by 2 with adding 5.

G. Add 1, add 2, add 3, etc.

H. Multiply by 3.

I. Divide by 2.

J. Alternate subtracting 4 with adding 3.

1. 6, 13, 20, 27, _____, …

2. 4, 12, 36, 108, _____, …

3. 30, 10, 60, 20, _____, …

4. 100, 85, 75, 60, _____, …

5. 11, 22, 44, 77, _____, …

6. 24, 20, 23, 19, 22, _____, …

7. 10, 19, 28, 37, 46, _____, …

8. 2, 3, 5, 8, 12, _____, …

9. 3, 6, 11, _____, 27, 54, _____, …

10. 96, _____, 24, 12, _____, 3, …

Finding the Right Combinations

Help Detective Doogan find the locked-up goods. Fill in each table with the missing input or output numbers.

1.

x	3x
5	◯
7	◯
9	◯
12	◯

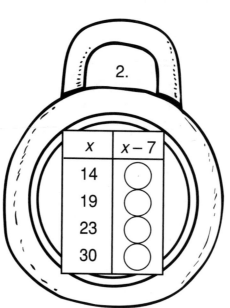

2.

x	x − 7
14	◯
19	◯
23	◯
30	◯

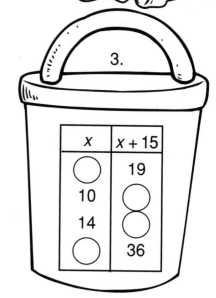

3.

x	x + 15
◯	19
10	◯
14	◯
◯	36

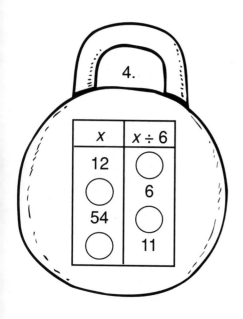

4.

x	x ÷ 6
12	◯
◯	6
54	◯
◯	11

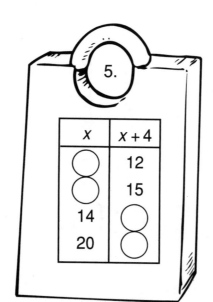

5.

x	x + 4
◯	12
◯	15
14	◯
20	◯

6.

x	9x
◯	27
5	◯
◯	63
10	◯

Name _____

Finding the Right Combinations

Help Detective Doogan find the locked-up goods. Fill in each table with the missing input or output numbers. Next, add the circled numbers in each table. Find that sum in the riddle below. Write the matching lock's letter on the line.

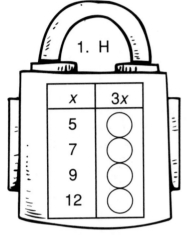

1. H

x	3x
5	◯
7	◯
9	◯
12	◯

2. D

x	x − 7
14	◯
19	◯
23	◯
30	◯

3. S

x	x + 15
◯	19
10	◯
14	◯
◯	36

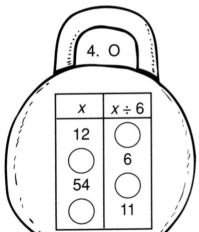

4. O

x	x ÷ 6
12	◯
◯	6
54	◯
◯	11

5. U

x	x + 4
◯	12
◯	15
14	◯
20	◯

6. G

x	9x
◯	27
5	◯
◯	63
10	◯

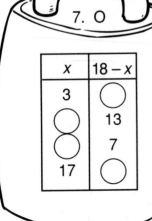

7. O

x	18 − x
3	◯
◯	13
◯	7
17	◯

8. E

x	x ÷ 8
16	◯
32	◯
◯	7
◯	12

Where are the hidden goods?
In the...

___ ___ ___ ___ ___ ___ ___ ___!
58   113 145 99   32   61   79   158

Password, Please!

Read the rule. Then complete the table. The first one has been done for you.

1.
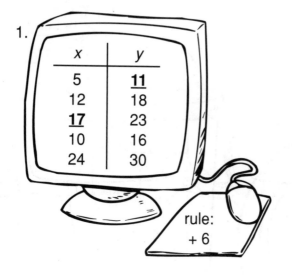

x	y
5	**11**
12	18
17	23
10	16
24	30

rule: + 6

2.

x	y
4	
9	72
10	80
	64
3	24

rule: x 8

3.
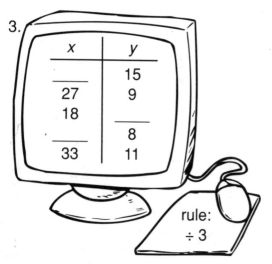

x	y
	15
27	9
18	
	8
33	11

rule: ÷ 3

4.
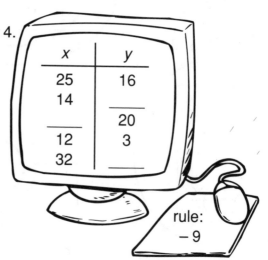

x	y
25	16
14	
	20
12	3
32	

rule: − 9

5.
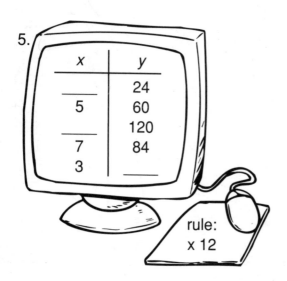

x	y
	24
5	60
	120
7	84
3	

rule: x 12

6.
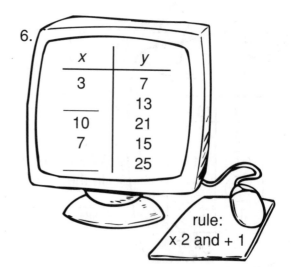

x	y
3	7
	13
10	21
7	15
	25

rule: x 2 and + 1

Password, Please!

Determine the rule. Then complete the table. The first one has been done for you.

1.

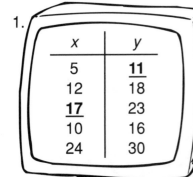

x	y
5	**11**
12	18
17	23
10	16
24	30

rule: **+ 6**

2.

x	y
4	
9	72
10	80
	64
3	24

rule: _____

3.

x	y
	15
27	9
18	
	8
33	11

rule: _____

4.

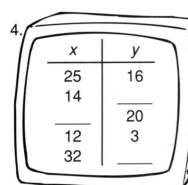

x	y
25	16
14	
	20
12	3
32	

rule: _____

5.

x	y
	24
5	60
	120
7	84
3	

rule: _____

6.

x	y
3	7
	13
10	21
7	15
	25

hint: x and +

rule: _____

7.

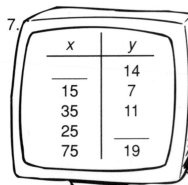

x	y
	14
15	7
35	11
25	
75	19

hint: ÷ and +

rule: _____

8.

x	y
13	5
	8
35	16
27	
9	3

hint: − and ÷

rule: _____

9.

x	y
	53
6	29
15	
	21
8	37

hint: x and +

rule: _____

Answer Keys

Page 6
A. Sandwiches come in many forms.
D. Picnics are enjoyable anywhere and at almost any time.
E. Owning a pet is a big responsibility.
G. Children should eat healthy foods.

Page 7
Topic sentences will vary. Accept reasonable responses.

Pages 8 and 9
Answers will vary. Accept reasonable responses.

Page 10

Singular	Plural	Rule
boy	boys	4
berry	berries	3
pencil	pencils	1
tax	taxes	2
monkey	monkeys	4
church	churches	2
wish	wishes	2
gas	gases	2
turkey	turkeys	4
chair	chairs	1
sky	skies	3
clock	clocks	1
candy	candies	3
butterfly	butterflies	3

Page 11

Singular	Plural	Rule
boy	boys	4
berry	berries	3
goose	geese	7
pencil	pencils	1
tax	taxes	2
shelf	shelves	6
veto	vetoes	5
monkey	monkeys	4
tooth	teeth	7
knife	knives	6
patio	patios	5
church	churches	2
wish	wishes	2
half	halves	6
gas	gases	2
turkey	turkeys	4
tomato	tomatoes	5
chair	chairs	1
sky	skies	3
mouse	mice	7
clock	clocks	1
candy	candies	3
foot	feet	7
butterfly	butterflies	3
zero	zeros	5

Pages 12 and 13

1. year's
2. contestants
3. tonight's
4. school's
5. members
6. boys'
7. drinks
8. students
9. contestants'
10. awards
11. winner's
12. Mr. Davidson's

Page 14

We loves fresh strawberries.	(We love fresh strawberries.)	2
(Good drivers buckle up!)	Good drivers buckles up!	2
(Ice cream tastes great!)	Ice cream taste great!	1
The bridge freeze before the road.	(The bridge freezes before the road.)	1
We writes messages on T-shirts while you wait!	(We write messages on T-shirts while you wait!)	2
(Local runner wins big race!)	Local runner win big race!	1
Used cars runs well!	(Used cars run well!)	2
I buys old stamps.	(I buy old stamps.)	2
(The road curves to the left.)	The road curve to the left.	1
(Mechanic needs assistant.)	Mechanic need assistant.	1
(We sell for less!)	We sells for less!	2
All vehicles drives slowly around the curve.	(All vehicles drive slowly around the curve.)	2
Dr. Dolan welcome new patients.	(Dr. Dolan welcomes new patients.)	1
(Attorney Tommy Thompson fights for you!)	Attorney Tommy Thompson fight for you!	1

Page 15

We loves fresh strawberries.	*We love fresh strawberries.*	2
Good drivers buckles up!	Good drivers buckle up!	2
Ice cream taste great!	Ice cream tastes great!	1
The bridge freeze before the road.	The bridge freezes before the road.	1
We writes messages on T-shirts while you wait!	We write messages on T-shirts while you wait!	2
Local marathon runner win big race!	Local marathon runner wins big race!	1
Used cars runs well!	Used cars run well!	2
I buys old stamps.	I buy old stamps.	2
The road curve to the left.	The road curves to the left.	1
Mechanic need assistant.	Mechanic needs assistant.	1
We sells for less!	We sell for less!	2
All vehicles drives slowly around the curve.	All vehicles drive slowly around the curve.	2
Dr. Dolan welcome new patients.	Dr. Dolan welcomes new patients.	1
Attorney Tommy Thompson fight for you!	Attorney Tommy Thompson fights for you!	1

Page 16

Nouns	Pronouns	Verbs
afternoon	they	raked
houses	Everyone	whistled
leaves	She	studying
Washington, DC		wanted
parents		volunteered

Adjectives	Adverbs
brisk	quickly
small	loudly
harder	

Page 17

Nouns	Pronouns	Verbs
afternoon	they	raked
houses	Everyone	whistled
leaves	She	studying
Washington, DC		wanted
parents		volunteered
sale		thought

Adjectives	Adverbs
brisk	quickly
raked	loudly
small	desperately
Several	eagerly
harder	

Page 18

1. The porcupine climbed (over) the dead |tree|.
2. The angry porcupine hit the animal (with) its |tail|.
3. Two porcupines ate the flowers (for) a |snack|.
4. Porcupines can't shoot quills (at) their |enemies|.
5. Some porcupines can hang (by) their |tails|.
6. Those porcupines came (from) the |zoo|.
7. The porcupine moved slowly (through) the |forest|.
8. A porcupine can strip the bark (off) a |tree|.
9. Two porcupines took a nap (in) a hollow |log|.
10. A porcupine's tail is packed (with) sharp |quills|.

Page 19

Part 1

1. The porcupine climbed (over) the dead |tree|.
2. The angry porcupine hit the animal (with) its |tail|.
3. Two porcupines ate the flowers (for) a |snack|.
4. Porcupines can't shoot quills (at) their |enemies|.
5. Some porcupines can hang (by) their |tails|.
6. Those porcupines came (from) the |zoo|.
7. The porcupine moved slowly (through) the |forest|.
8. A porcupine can strip the bark (off) a |tree|.
9. Two porcupines took a nap (in) a hollow |log|.
10. A porcupine's tail is packed (with) sharp |quills|.

Part 2
Answers will vary.

Pages 20 and 21

Sentences will vary. Accept reasonable responses.

Page 22
1. compound
2. simple
3. simple
4. compound
5. simple
6. compound
7. simple
8. compound
9. compound
10. compound

Your appetite!

Page 23
1. compound
2. simple
3. simple
4. compound
5. simple
6. compound
7. compound
8. simple
9. compound
10. simple
11. compound
12. compound

Your appetite!

Page 24
Answers may vary. Possible answers include the following:

1. I want to renovate my kitchen. I need new appliances and a new floor. Can you please give me an estimate? My number is 555-0198.
2. Harriet, please come quickly! My dishwasher is broken, and suds are filling up my kitchen.
3. The wallpaper in my bathroom is peeling. Please call me at 555-0189. I hope you can fix it soon. I am having guests on Friday.
4. Do you fix toilets? Mine has been leaking. I think the water will ruin the new tile if the toilet is not repaired soon.

Page 25
Answers may vary. Possible answers include the following:

1. I want to renovate my kitchen. I need new appliances and a new floor. Can you please give me an estimate? My number is 555-0198.
2. correct
3. Harriet, please come quickly! My dishwasher is broken, and suds are filling up my kitchen.
4. The wallpaper in my bathroom is peeling. Please call me at 555-0189. I hope you can fix it soon. I am having guests on Friday.
5. correct
6. Do you fix toilets? Mine has been leaking. I think the water will ruin the new tile if the toilet is not repaired soon.

Page 26
Answers may vary. Accept reasonable responses.

Egg Coloring Kit
Drop one color tablet into a small amount of vinegar. Mix until dissolved and add a cup of cold water.

Easy-to-Assemble Table
Flip the table so the legs meet the floor and the flat surface faces the ceiling. Press firmly on the table to test its strength before placing heavy objects on it.

Jam and Jelly Cleaning Kit
Clean the inside top rim of the container. While the contents are hot, cover with a ⅛-inch layer of melted wax. When the contents have cooled, add another layer of melted wax. Tilt and rotate the jar to seal it completely.

Page 27
Answers may vary. Accept reasonable responses.

Egg Coloring Kit
Fill a pan with water. Hard-boil eggs in the water and let the eggs cool. Drop one color tablet into a small amount of vinegar. Mix until dissolved and add a cup of cold water. Lower an egg into the colored water and wait until it is the color you desire. Leave it in the solution longer for a brighter color. Drain and place the eggs in a tray. Leave them in the tray until they are completely dry.

Easy-to-Assemble Table
Remove the table from the box. Remove the plastic cover and throw it away. Place the table on a smooth surface so that the legs are facing you. Firmly move one leg until it meets the table at a 90-degree angle and you hear it snap into place. Repeat this process with the other three legs. Flip the table so the legs meet the floor and the flat surface faces the ceiling. Press firmly on the table to test its strength before placing heavy objects on it.

Jam and Jelly Canning Kit
This wax is perfect for sealing jars, using in open-topped containers, and making candles. To use the wax in preserving your jams and jellies, fill glasses or jars to within one-half inch of the top. Clean the inside top rim of the container. While the contents are hot, cover with a ⅛-inch layer of melted wax. When the contents have cooled, add another layer of melted wax. Tilt and rotate the jar to seal it completely.

Page 28
Halloween
Moss Street
England
Big Pigeon River
October
Atlantic Ocean
Mrs. Crabtree
Wednesday
American Revolution
Kentucky

It was her shadow.

Page 29
Halloween
American Red Cross
Moss Street
England
Big Pigeon River
Beverly Cleary
October
Atlantic Ocean
Mrs. Crabtree
Wednesday
American Revolution
The Charlotte Chronicle
Kentucky
Jupiter

It was her shadow.

Page 30

NC 1. Welcome back to another school year at Oddville Elementary!
NC 2. We have much to look forward to in the next ten months.
1 3. We have added four new elective classes, two new teachers, and three new clubs.
2 4. We are sad that Mr. Milligan retired, but we welcome a new teacher in his place.
2 5. We have improved our lunch program by adding ice cream to every menu, and we have added comfortable new padded stools to the lunchroom tables.
2 6. Our playground has received a new coat of paint on all the old equipment, and we have added a state-of-the-art skateboard park!
NC 7. Our teachers and staff are rested and eager to work with parents and students this year.
NC 8. Each student is required to bring his or her own supplies to class on the first day of school.
1 9. You will need two green folders with frog pictures on the front, six rainbow pencils, a blue crayon, and scissors.
1 10. You will also need an umbrella, a funnel, a fork, a bag of cotton balls, two toothpicks, and six medium rubber bands.

Page 31

NC 1. Welcome back to another school year at Oddville Elementary!
NC 2. We have much to look forward to in the next ten months.
2 3. In fact, this promises to be our very best school year ever!
1 4. We have added four new elective classes, two new teachers, and three new clubs.
3 5. We are sad that Mr. Milligan retired, but we welcome a new teacher in his place.
3 6. We have improved our lunch program by adding ice cream to every menu, and we have added comfortable new padded stools to the lunchroom tables.
3 7. Our playground has received a new coat of paint on all the old equipment, and we have added a state-of-the-art skateboard park!
NC 8. Our teachers and staff are rested and eager to work with parents and students this year.
2 9. In short, welcome back!
NC 10. Each student is required to bring his or her own supplies to class on the first day of school.
1 11. You will need two green folders with frog pictures on the front, six rainbow pencils, a blue crayon, and scissors.
1 12. You will also need an umbrella, a funnel, a fork, a bag of cotton balls, two toothpicks, and six medium rubber bands.

Pages 32 and 33

1. Sara said, "I think we should allow students to attend school over the Internet."
2. Taking a card from the suggestion box, Tara said, "A fifth grader suggests that we start school later in the day. He thinks ten o'clock would be a good time to start."
3. Mark said, "We should be able to buy soft drinks at lunch."
4. Marla added, "My dad is a nutritionist, and it would be a good idea for students to have a mid-morning and a mid-afternoon snack each day."
5. When it was her turn to speak, Candi said, "I think a pet-obedience elective class would be awesome."
6. "My mom thinks it would be a good idea if the school buses took kids straight to soccer practice in the afternoon," added Lydia.
7. "I agree with your suggestion," said Randall.
8. "We should have more time during class to work on homework and projects so our afternoons are free," offered Louise.
9. Sara said, "I think we should have sofas and comfortable chairs added to the lunchroom for relaxing after we eat."
10. At the end of the meeting, Kayla said, "I don't think we should make any changes. I like school just the way it is."

Page 34

Part 1:
1. indirect
2. indirect
3. direct
4. direct
5. indirect
6. direct
7. direct

Part 2:
8. "I guess it would be a good idea to bring pets to school," said Ms. Marcy Darcy, "but who will clean up after them?"
9. Miss Kneiss asked, "Which class would we drop so that we could add soccer practice? What about the kids who don't play soccer? What class would they take?"
10. Principal Garvey said, "We'll take a vote at our next meeting."

Page 35

Part 1:
1. indirect
2. indirect
3. direct
4. direct
5. indirect
6. direct
7. direct

Part 2:
8. direct; "I guess it would be a good idea to bring pets to school," said Ms. Marcy Darcy, "but who will clean up after them?"
9. indirect
10. direct; Miss Kneiss asked, "Which class would we drop so that we could add soccer practice? What about the kids who don't play soccer? What class would they take?"
11. indirect
12. direct; Principal Garvey said, "We'll take a vote at our next meeting."

Page 36

The following sentences needed corrections:
1. Will and his new friends arrived early to the school's Fall Festival.
3. First, they went to the art club's booth to make a scarecrow.
5. Jan won a prize coupon in Mr. Bumble's balloon-sit game.
7. No matter how hard he tried, Will just couldn't seem to win a prize.
8. Will and Jan had fun in the P.E. teacher's Old Clothes Relay.
9. He had a great time at the pumpkin seed–spitting booth, but he still didn't win a prize.

Extra HOMEWORK for one week!

Page 37

The following sentences needed corrections:
1. Will and his new friends arrived early to the school's Fall Festival.
3. First, they went to the art club's booth to make a scarecrow.
4. Will's stomach did a flip when he saw a spider on the floor.
6. Jan won a prize coupon in Mr. Bumble's balloon-sit game.
8. No matter how hard he tried, Will just couldn't seem to win a prize.
9. Will and Jan had fun in the P.E. teacher's Old Clothes Relay.
10. He had a great time at the pumpkin seed–spitting booth, but he still didn't win a prize.
13. After that, Will decided that just hangin' around and having a good time was the best prize of all!

Extra HOMEWORK for one week!

Page 38

Dear tim,

how are you? I am finally all settled in at our new house. it is smaller than our old one, but at least it has a pool.

i am getting used to my new school. My teacher's name is Ms. sherry berry, and she is very nice. There are 22 other kids in my class. I have two new friends. their names are Beau Monroe and Jan Haversham. We are in dogsledding class together.

We have some class pets. We have two fish, some crickets, a baby porcupine, and a ten-foot-long python. It was hard to concentrate at first with Pal slithering around on the floor. He's pretty friendly though, so I hardly notice him now. I just try not to drop my pencil.

That's about all the news I have for now. My speed-typing club meets every Thursday, so I'll type you again soon. Tell everyone hello and write soon.

Your friend,

Will McGill

Page 39

Dear tim⌄

⌄how are you❓I am finally all settled in at our new house. ⌄it is smaller than our old one⌄ but at least it has a pool⊙

⌄i am getting used to my new school. My teacher's name is Ms. sherry berry⌄ and she is very nice. There are 22 other kids in my class⊙ I have two new friends⊙ their names are Beau Monroe and Jan Haversham. We are in dogsledding class together.

We have some class pets. We have two fish⌄ some crickets⌄ a baby porcupine⌄ and a ten-foot-long python. It was hard to concentrate at first with Pal slithering around on the floor⊙ He's pretty friendly though⌄ so I hardly notice him now. I just try not to drop my pencil❗

That's about all the news I have for now. My speed-typing club meets every Thursday, so I'll type you again soon. Tell everyone hello and write soon.

Your friend⌄

Will McGill

Page 40

Answers may vary. Accept any words in which the prefixes and suffixes are used correctly.

dislike, unlike
enjoyable, enjoyment
disagree
lovely, loveable, loveless, lover
rewind, unwind, overwind
foreman, superman
childhood, childish, childless
happier, happily, happiness, happiest

joyful, joyless, joyous
discourage
cheerful, cheerless
disprove
thankful, thankless
hopeful, hopeless
kindest, kindly, kindness, kinder
movement, moveable, mover

Page 41

Answers may vary. Accept any words in which the prefixes and suffixes are used correctly.

teacher, teachable
enjoyable, enjoyment
disagree
counteract, exact, react, transact
dislike, unlike
foreman, superman
childhood, childish, childless
lovely, loveable, loveless, lover
rewind, unwind, overwind
transport, deport, export, import, teleport
cheerful, cheerless
happier, happily, happiness, happiest

joyful, joyless, joyous
redo, undo, overdo
workable, worker
readable, reader
thankful, thankless
discourage
kindest, kindly, kindness, kinder
disprove
re-create, procreate, miscreate
hopeful, hopeless
repress, express, depress
movement, moveable, mover

Page 42

Answers may vary. Possible answers include the following:
superb
excellent
finest
understand
quickly
terrible
reasonable
adores
super
huge

Page 43

Answers will vary. Accept reasonable responses.

Pages 44 and 45

1. public
2. pleasure
3. lenient
4. assure
5. decorate
6. lament
7. uncouth
8. scarcity
9. idle
10. proceed
11. agitate
12. desirable

Page 46

3	D	a material that covers the face or head	1	A	a place to keep money
5	A	a group of one kind of animal	5	D	a tool used to make something smooth
1	D	to bend low as a sign of respect	6	D	a young boy or girl
1	D	the front of a ship	3	D	something that hides
4	A	new or unusual	7	A	a certain day, month, or year
7	A	a get-together with a friend	5	A	to gather in a crowd
			2	D	to hold in place
6	D	to tease or joke	1	A	a mound
5	D	a box or folder that keeps papers	4	A	a long book with a made-up story
2	D	a weight used to keep a ship in place			

Page 47

3	D	a material that covers the face or head	7	D	a material used to keep something tightly closed
5	A	a group of one kind of animal			
10	A	something you work toward	1	A	a place to keep money
1	D	to bend low as a sign of respect	5	D	a tool used to make something smooth
7	D	a mammal that spends most of its time in water	8	A	a certain day, month, or year
9	A	the best or highest point	6	D	a young boy or girl
1	D	the front of a ship	9	A	the highest part of a mountain
4	A	new or unusual	3	D	something that hides
8	A	a get-together with a friend	5	A	to gather in a crowd
			2	D	to hold in place
6	D	to tease or joke	10	A	a net on a frame, used in sports
5	D	a box or folder that keeps papers	1	A	a mound
2	D	a weight used to keep a ship in place	4	A	a long book with a made-up story

Page 48

1. S
2. S
3. M
4. M
5. M
6. S
7. S
8. M
9. S
10. S

Page 49

Sentences will vary. Accept reasonable responses.

1. S; Monica is a pretty picture in her new dress.
2. S; Hannah's mind is a steel trap.
3. M; Lana is as smart as a wizard in math.
4. M; Jacob acted like a perfect angel at the party.
5. M; Naomi's closet looks like a junkyard!
6. S; Jeremy was a speeding bullet as he raced to catch the bus.
7. S; This book is a magic carpet, taking you to faraway lands.
8. M; You are like the sunshine in my life.
9. S; Her evening gown was a sparkling diamond.
10. S; Kyle's voice was a foghorn, piercing through the noisy crowd.

Page 50

1. Winning second and not first place was **nothing to sneeze at.**
2. Boy, Kyle was really **burned up!**
3. Daniel, could you please **lend me a hand?**
4. My granny is 80 years old, but she's **fit as a fiddle.**
5. Sue thought the reading test was **easy as pie.**
6. After he got his test score back, Zach looked **down in the dumps.**
7. My brother really **gets on my nerves.**
8. When his sister wouldn't hurry, Joey tried **to keep his shirt on.**
9. Dillon, if you agree with me, then **put your John Hancock here.**

Page 51

1. Winning second and not first place was **nothing to sneeze at.**
2. Boy, Kyle was really **burned up!**
3. Daniel, could you please **lend me a hand?**
4. My granny is 80 years old, but she's **fit as a fiddle.**
5. Sue thought the reading test was **easy as pie.**
6. After he got his test score back, Zach looked **down in the dumps.**
7. My brother really **gets on my nerves.**
8. When his sister wouldn't hurry, Joey tried **to keep his shirt on.**
9. Dillon, if you agree with me, then **put your John Hancock here.**
10. When it comes to giving a speech, I always **get cold feet.**
11. To get windows clean, you need to use a little **elbow grease.**
12. The teacher told Sharon to **hold her tongue.**

Page 52

1. facts
2. opinions
3. facts
4. opinions
5. facts
6. facts

Page 53

1. facts
2. opinions
3. facts
4. facts
5. opinions
6. facts
7. opinions
8. facts
9. facts

Page 54

1. C
2. F
3. B
4. A
5. E
6. D
7. G

Page 55

1. D
2. G
3. B
4. A
5. F
6. E
7. H
8. I
9. C
10. J

Pages 56 and 57

Alligators
- shy
- prefer to eat animals like rabbits, snakes, deer, pigs, and birds
- heavyset body
- wide, blunt snout
- live in freshwater environments

Both
- part of the crocodilian reptile group
- cold-blooded
- live in warm climates
- lay eggs
- scaly skin
- awkward on land
- masters of the water
- can close off their noses, throats, and ears when they dive

Crocodiles
- mean hunters
- will eat humans
- slender body
- long, pointed snout
- live in calm saltwater environments

Page 58

1. b
2. a
3. a
4. b
5. b
6. b

Page 59

Answers will vary. Accept reasonable responses.
1. Starlett is very close to her family.
2. Starlett has lived in many places.
3. Starlett has not always wanted to be an actress.
4. Starlett O'Hair is known for having fancy hairstyles.
5. Starlett hopes to have a long acting career.
6. Starlett has many hobbies.

Page 60

Topic: "Trained Animals"
Main Idea: g
Supporting Details: b, d, h (Order of answers may vary.)

Topic: "Daring Acts"
Main Idea: c
Supporting Details: a, e, f (Order of answers may vary.)

Page 61

Topic: One possible answer is "Trained Animals."
Main Idea: h
Supporting Details: b, d, i (Order of answers may vary.)

Topic: One possible answer is "Daring Acts."
Main Idea: c
Supporting Details: a, e, g (Order of answers may vary.)

Pages 62 and 63
1. Answers may vary. Answers should include that the passage describes how experts find information about Columbus.
2. Experts put the facts together like a puzzle.
3. a. T
   b. N
   c. F
4. Answers may vary. Accept reasonable responses. A possible answer is the following:
   Experts make history by putting facts together piece by piece. Columbus also made history with his voyage to the New World.
5. b

Pages 64 and 65
Answers may vary. Accept reasonable responses.

1. People came to the Arctic from England, Portugal, Spain, France, and Russia. Lines C and G.
2. Europeans came to the Arctic looking for a northwest passage; to fish for cod and herring; to trade for fox, mink, and beaver furs; and to hunt whales. Lines B, C, D, and L.
3. The Inuit traded for wooden boats, iron screws, knives, woven cloth, fishing hooks, nets, and guns. Lines G, H, I, and J.
4. The Inuit got metal tools instead of having to make tools out of bone and stone. Fish hooks, nets, and guns made fishing and hunting easier. Lines I and J.
5. The Inuit trapped animals just for their fur, so animals became harder to find. The Inuit began to give up old ways. Many Inuit died from diseases such as smallpox, measles, and the flu. Lines K, M, N, O, and P.
6. The Inuit moved closer to the trading posts because it was harder to find animals and they needed the European goods. Lines M and N.

Page 66
1. C
2. G
3. D
4. J
5. A
6. F
7. E
8. I
9. B
10. H

Page 67
1. D
2. H
3. L
4. A
5. F
6. O
7. I
8. E
9. B
10. G
11. K
12. J
13. N
14. C
15. M

Page 68
Scene 1: B
Scene 2: A
Scene 3: A
Scene 4: B

Page 69
Answers will vary. Possible answers include the following:
Scene 1: Jenna looks outside and realizes a bad storm is approaching.
Scene 2: Jenna searches for Brian.
Scene 3: Jenna struggles to get Brian and herself to safety.
Scene 4: Jenna and her parents are happy to be reunited.

Page 70
1. a
2. b
3. b
4. c
5. c
6. c
7. a
8. a

Page 71
1. a
2. b
3. b
4. d
5. c
6. c
7. a
8. d

Page 72
1. no
2. no
3. Students should list three of the five answers: 1998, 1994, 1990, 1986, 1982.
4. 2000
5. 1992
6. More Americans seem to exercise their right to vote during presidential election years.
7. 36,789,579
8. Answers will vary.

Page 73
1. no
2. no
3. Students should list three of the five answers: 1998, 1994, 1990, 1986, 1982.
4. 2000
5. 1992
6. More Americans seem to exercise their right to vote during presidential election years.
7. 36,789,579
8. Answers will vary.
9. Answers will vary.
10. Answers will vary.

Page 74
1. gander
   gangly
   gangplank
   gape
   garbage
2. siding
   sight
   silence
   silent
   silky
3. huff
   huge
   hula
   hulk
   humble
4. model
   modem
   mohair
   moisture
   moldy
5. badminton
   baffle
   balk
   ball
   ballet
6. plenty
   plight
   plot
   plow
   plum

Page 75

1. gander
   gangly
   gangplank
   gangway
   gape
   garbage

2. siding
   sift
   sight
   signal
   silence
   silent
   silky

3. huff
   huge
   hula
   hulk
   hullabaloo
   humble

4. mock
   model
   modem
   mohair
   moist
   moisture
   moldy

5. backstroke
   badminton
   baffle
   balk
   ball
   ballet

6. plenty
   pliers
   plight
   plot
   plow
   plug
   plum

Page 76

1. 2
2. 1
3. 2
4. 1
5. 1
6. 4
7. 1
8. 3
9. 2
10. 3

Page 77

1. 2
2. 1
3. 2
4. 1
5. 1
6. 4
7. 1
8. 3
9. 2
10. 3
11. 2
12. 3
13. 1
14. 2
15. 2

Page 78

1. C
2. A
3. E
4. C
5. B
6. D
7. A
8. E

Page 79

A. dictionary—a book that lists words alphabetically and explains the meanings, spellings, uses, and pronunciations of words
B. thesaurus—a type of dictionary that lists words alphabetically along with their synonyms and other related words, such as antonyms
C. atlas—a book of maps
D. encyclopedia—a book or set of books that lists subjects alphabetically and provides significant information about each subject
E. almanac—an annually published resource that contains information about particular subjects

1. C
2. A
3. E
4. C
5. D
6. B
7. D
8. A
9. C
10. E

Page 80

1. TTh
2. H
3. T
4. O
5. HTh
6. TTh
7. H
8. TTh
9. Th
10. H
11. O
12. Th
13. H
14. Th
15. HTh

Page 81

1. TTh
2. H
3. T
4. O
5. HTh
6. TTh
7. H
8. TTh
9. Th
10. H
11. O
12. Th
13. H
14. Th
15. HTh
16. O
17. H
18. HTh
19. H
20. O

Page 82

1. correct
2. incorrect
3. correct
4. correct
5. incorrect
6. incorrect
7. incorrect
8. correct
9. correct
10. incorrect
11. correct
12. incorrect

The new slogan is WIDGETS ROCK!

Page 83

1. correct
2. incorrect
3. correct
4. correct
5. incorrect
6. incorrect
7. incorrect
8. correct
9. correct
10. incorrect
11. correct
12. incorrect
13. incorrect
14. correct
15. correct
16. correct
17. incorrect
18. incorrect

The new slogan is WIDGETS WORK WONDERS!

Page 84

1. 256
2. 175
3. 2,244
4. 180
5. 2,808
6. 576
7. 490
8. 2,145
9. 1,524
10. 469
11. 609
12. 2,715
13. 3,222
14. 235
15. 78

The EGYPTIAN EXHIBIT.

Page 85

1. 256
2. 425
3. 2,244
4. 480
5. 2,808
6. 576
7. 1,960
8. 16,445
9. 1,524
10. 469
11. 1,827
12. 27,150
13. 3,222
14. 235
15. 728

The EGYPTIAN EXHIBIT.

154

Page 86

1. 24 R1
2. 17
3. 20 R5
4. 13 R3
5. 38 R4
6. 25
7. 188 R3
8. 21
9. 14
10. 138 R2
11. 36 R1
12. 38 R1

Tom and Tina spent $20.00 on souvenirs.

Page 87

1. 24 R1
2. 17
3. 32 R4
4. 20 R5
5. 31 R5
6. 13 R3
7. 38 R4
8. 25
9. 188 R3
10. 21
11. 14
12. 138 R2
13. 21 R7
14. 36 R1
15. 151 R5
16. 38 R1

Tom and Tina spent $41.00 on souvenirs.

Page 88

ones	**hundredths**	tenths
tenths	hundredths	**ones**
hundredths	tenths	**ones**
ones	**tenths**	hundredths
tenths	ones	hundredths
hundredths	tenths	ones
hundredths	**ones**	tenths
hundredths	**ones**	tenths
ones	**tenths**	hundredths
tenths	**hundredths**	ones
ones	tenths	**hundredths**
hundredths	tenths	**ones**
hundredths	**tenths**	ones
hundredths	ones	**tenths**
ones	hundredths	**tenths**

Decimal Dude had a ten-ounce T-bone for dinner.

Page 89

ones	**hundredths**	thousandths	tenths
tenths	thousandths	**ones**	hundredths
hundredths	thousandths	**ones**	tenths
thousandths	ones	**tenths**	hundredths
ones	**thousandths**	hundredths	tenths
hundredths	tenths	ones	thousandths
thousandths	ones	tenths	hundredths
hundredths	**ones**	thousandths	tenths
ones	**tenths**	hundredths	thousandths
tenths	**hundredths**	thousandths	ones
thousandths	tenths	**hundredths**	ones
hundredths	thousandths	**ones**	tenths
tenths	**thousandths**	ones	hundredths
thousandths	ones	**tenths**	hundredths
ones	hundredths	tenths	**thousandths**

Decimal Dude had a ten-ounce T-bone for dinner.

Page 90

1. $\frac{1}{2}$ is red.
2. $\frac{3}{5}$ is yellow.
3. $\frac{1}{6}$ is not red.
4. $\frac{5}{9}$ is colored.
5. $\frac{8}{8}$, or 1, is green.
6. $\frac{5}{8}$ is not red.
7. $\frac{0}{3}$, or 0, is yellow.
8. $\frac{5}{6}$ is green or red.

Page 91

1. $\frac{1}{2}$ is red.
2. $\frac{3}{5}$ is yellow.
3. $\frac{1}{6}$ is not red.
4. $\frac{5}{9}$ is colored.
5. $\frac{8}{8}$, or 1, is green.
6. $\frac{5}{8}$ is not red.
7. $\frac{0}{3}$, or 0, is yellow.
8. $\frac{5}{6}$ is green or red.
9.

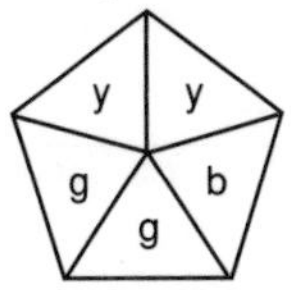

10.

br	br	br
br	br	br
br	o	g
g	g	g

11.

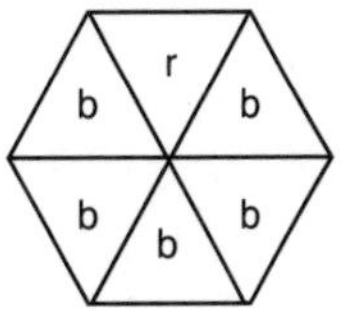

12.

o	o
o	b
b	b
g	g
g	r

Page 92

1. $\frac{5}{10}$, $\frac{1}{2}$
2. $\frac{1}{3}$, $\frac{3}{9}$
3. $\frac{1}{4}$, $\frac{4}{16}$
4. $\frac{6}{9}$, $\frac{2}{3}$
5. $\frac{1}{4}$, $\frac{9}{36}$
6. $\frac{6}{10}$, $\frac{3}{5}$
7. $\frac{4}{5}$, $\frac{20}{25}$
8. $\frac{6}{10}$, $\frac{12}{20}$
9. $\frac{3}{24}$, $\frac{1}{8}$

Page 93

1. $\frac{5}{10}$, $\frac{1}{2}$
2. $\frac{1}{3}$, $\frac{3}{9}$
3. $\frac{1}{4}$, $\frac{4}{16}$
4. $\frac{6}{9}$, $\frac{2}{3}$
5. $\frac{1}{4}$, $\frac{9}{36}$
6. $\frac{6}{10}$, $\frac{3}{5}$
7. $\frac{4}{5}$, $\frac{20}{25}$
8. $\frac{6}{10}$, $\frac{12}{20}$
9. $\frac{3}{24}$, $\frac{1}{8}$
10. $\frac{2}{7}$, $\frac{8}{28}$
11. $\frac{3}{4}$, $\frac{12}{16}$
12. $\frac{7}{14}$, $\frac{1}{2}$

Page 94

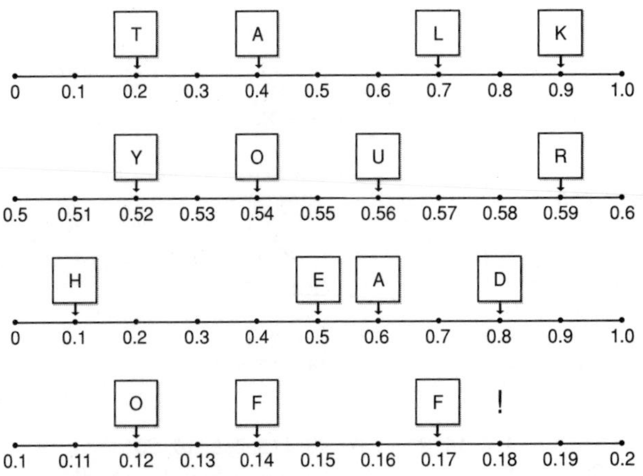

Page 95

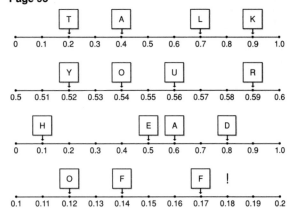

Page 96

The following problems should be colored:

$\frac{1}{3} + \frac{1}{3} = \frac{2}{3}$

$\frac{4}{5} - \frac{2}{5} = \frac{2}{5}$

$\frac{7}{8} - \frac{2}{8} = \frac{5}{8}$

$\frac{2}{8} + \frac{2}{8} = \frac{4}{8}$

$\frac{3}{10} + \frac{3}{10} = \frac{6}{10}$

$\frac{2}{4} + \frac{1}{4} = \frac{3}{4}$

$\frac{5}{10} - \frac{3}{10} = \frac{2}{10}$

Page 97

The following problems should be colored:

$\frac{1}{3} + \frac{1}{3} = \frac{2}{3}$

$\frac{3}{7} + \frac{2}{7} = \frac{5}{7}$

$\frac{4}{5} - \frac{2}{5} = \frac{2}{5}$

$\frac{1}{2} - \frac{1}{2} = 0$

$\frac{2}{8} + \frac{2}{8} = \frac{4}{8}$

$\frac{5}{9} - \frac{2}{9} = \frac{3}{9}$

$\frac{7}{8} - \frac{2}{8} = \frac{5}{8}$

$\frac{3}{10} + \frac{3}{10} = \frac{6}{10}$

$\frac{2}{4} + \frac{1}{4} = \frac{3}{4}$

$\frac{5}{10} - \frac{3}{10} = \frac{2}{10}$

Page 98

1. $\frac{1}{8} + \frac{3}{4} = \frac{7}{8}$
   $\frac{1}{4} + \frac{1}{3} = \frac{7}{12}$

2. $\frac{1}{4} + \frac{2}{8} = \frac{1}{2}$
   $\frac{1}{10} + \frac{4}{5} = \frac{9}{10}$

3. $\frac{4}{9} - \frac{1}{3} = \frac{1}{9}$
   $\frac{3}{4} + \frac{1}{6} = \frac{11}{12}$

4. $\frac{2}{3} + \frac{1}{6} = \frac{5}{6}$
   $\frac{1}{4} + \frac{1}{6} = \frac{5}{12}$

5. $\frac{2}{5} + \frac{1}{2} = \frac{9}{10}$
   $\frac{1}{2} - \frac{2}{5} = \frac{1}{10}$

6. $\frac{4}{9} - \frac{1}{3} = \frac{1}{9}$
   $\frac{3}{8} + \frac{2}{16} = \frac{1}{2}$

Page 99

1. $\frac{1}{8} + \frac{3}{4} = \frac{7}{8}$
   $\frac{1}{12} + \frac{1}{2} = \frac{7}{12}$
   $\frac{1}{4} + \frac{1}{3} = \frac{7}{12}$

2. $\frac{1}{5} + \frac{3}{10} = \frac{1}{2}$
   $\frac{1}{4} + \frac{2}{8} = \frac{1}{2}$
   $\frac{1}{10} + \frac{4}{5} = \frac{9}{10}$

3. $\frac{4}{9} - \frac{1}{3} = \frac{1}{9}$
   $\frac{3}{4} + \frac{1}{6} = \frac{11}{12}$
   $\frac{5}{6} + \frac{1}{12} = \frac{11}{12}$

4. $\frac{2}{3} + \frac{1}{6} = \frac{5}{6}$
   $\frac{1}{4} + \frac{1}{6} = \frac{5}{12}$
   $\frac{3}{4} - \frac{2}{6} = \frac{5}{12}$

5. $\frac{2}{5} + \frac{1}{2} = \frac{9}{10}$
   $\frac{1}{2} - \frac{2}{5} = \frac{1}{10}$
   $\frac{4}{5} + \frac{1}{10} = \frac{9}{10}$

6. $\frac{4}{9} - \frac{1}{3} = \frac{1}{9}$
   $\frac{3}{9} + \frac{1}{6} = \frac{1}{2}$
   $\frac{3}{8} + \frac{2}{16} = \frac{1}{2}$

Page 100

1. 12: 1, 2, 3, 4, 6, 12
   15: 1, 3, 5, 15
   GCF: 3

2. 4: 1, 2, 4
   12: 1, 2, 3, 4, 6, 12
   GCF: 4

3. 9: 1, 3, 9
   18: 1, 2, 3, 6, 9, 18
   GCF: 9

4. 10: 1, 2, 5, 10
   25: 1, 5, 25
   GCF: 5

5. 4: 1, 2, 4
   14: 1, 2, 7, 14
   GCF: 2

6. 21: 1, 3, 7, 21
   27: 1, 3, 9, 27
   GCF: 3

7. 28: 1, 2, 4, 7, 14, 28
   35: 1, 5, 7, 35
   GCF: 7

8. 20: 1, 2, 4, 5, 10, 20
   30: 1, 2, 3, 5, 6, 10, 15, 30
   GCF: 10

9. 8: 1, 2, 4, 8
   12: 1, 2, 3, 4, 6, 12
   GCF: 4

Page 101

1. 12: 1, 2, 3, 4, 6, 12
   15: 1, 3, 5, 15
   GCF: 3

2. 12: 1, 2, 3, 4, 6, 12
   24: 1, 2, 3, 4, 6, 8, 12, 24
   GCF: 12

3. 9: 1, 3, 9
   18: 1, 2, 3, 6, 9, 18
   GCF: 9

4. 10: 1, 2, 5, 10
   25: 1, 5, 25
   GCF: 5

5. 4: 1, 2, 4
   14: 1, 2, 7, 14
   GCF: 2

6. 21: 1, 3, 7, 21
   49: 1, 7, 49
   GCF: 7

7. 28: 1, 2, 4, 7, 14, 28
   35: 1, 5, 7, 35
   GCF: 7

8. 20: 1, 2, 4, 5, 10, 20
   30: 1, 2, 3, 5, 6, 10, 15, 30
   GCF: 10

9. 8: 1, 2, 4, 8
   12: 1, 2, 3, 4, 6, 12
   GCF: 4

Page 102

	GOLD	RUBIES	
	PEARLS		

(R) $3\frac{1}{3}$ (P) $15\frac{1}{3}$ (O) $3\frac{3}{10}$ (B) $10\frac{2}{3}$

(I) $4\frac{2}{5}$ (G) $7\frac{9}{10}$ (S) $1\frac{1}{8}$ (S) $16\frac{5}{7}$

(E) $5\frac{2}{3}$ (U) $18\frac{7}{9}$ (R) $1\frac{1}{3}$ (L) $4\frac{7}{10}$

Page 103

	GOLD	RUBIES		
	PEARLS			

(R) $3\frac{1}{3}$ (P) $15\frac{2}{6}$ (O) $3\frac{3}{10}$ (B) $10\frac{2}{3}$ (E) $8\frac{1}{2}$

(I) $4\frac{2}{5}$ (G) $7\frac{9}{10}$ (S) $1\frac{1}{8}$ (S) $16\frac{5}{7}$ (D) $7\frac{1}{12}$

(E) $5\frac{2}{3}$ (U) $18\frac{7}{9}$ (R) $1\frac{1}{3}$ (L) $4\frac{7}{10}$ (L) $7\frac{5}{7}$

Page 104

1. $\frac{13}{5}$
2. $\frac{13}{12}$
3. $\frac{11}{3}$
4. $\frac{10}{3}$
5. $\frac{21}{4}$
6. $\frac{11}{6}$
7. $\frac{15}{2}$
8. $\frac{19}{6}$
9. $\frac{19}{4}$
10. $\frac{27}{5}$
11. $\frac{3}{2}$
12. $\frac{23}{3}$

A DOUGHNUT!

Page 105

1. $\frac{5}{2}$
2. $\frac{13}{5}$
3. $\frac{13}{12}$
4. $\frac{11}{3}$
5. $\frac{10}{3}$
6. $\frac{21}{4}$
7. $\frac{49}{8}$
8. $\frac{11}{6}$
9. $\frac{79}{8}$
10. $\frac{15}{2}$
11. $\frac{19}{6}$
12. $\frac{19}{4}$
13. $\frac{41}{10}$
14. $\frac{27}{5}$
15. $\frac{3}{2}$
16. $\frac{23}{3}$

A DOUGHNUT!

Page 106

1. 8:20 A.M.
2. 18 slices
3. $23.68

Page 107

1. 8:20 A.M.
2. 11:15 A.M.
3. 41 customers
4. 18 slices
5. $23.68

Page 108

1. 5 minstrels; 2 jugglers; 4 jesters
2. 92 vegetables; 50 fruits
3. 111 men; 67 women

Page 109

1. 5 minstrels; 2 jugglers; 4 jesters
2. 92 vegetables; 50 fruits
3. 111 men; 67 women
4. Monday: 16; Tuesday: 18; Wednesday: 19

Page 110

1.

Minutes	15	30	45	60	75	90	105	120
Specials	7	14	21	28	35	42	49	56

Solution: 28 specials, 56 specials

2.

Minutes	20	40	60	80	100	120	140	160
Orders	13	26	39	52	65	78	91	104

Solution: 39 orders, 2 hours 40 minutes

3.

Day	1	2	3	4	5	6	7	8	9	10	11	12	13	14
Chili				✓				✓				✓		
Chocolate pie			✓			✓			✓			✓		

Solution: 1 day

Page 111

1.

Minutes	15	30	45	60	75	90	105	120
Specials	7	14	21	28	35	42	49	56

Solution: 28 specials, 56 specials

2.

Minutes	20	40	60	80	100	120	140	160
Orders	13	26	39	52	65	78	91	104

Solution: 39 orders, 2 hours 40 minutes

3.

Day	1	2	3	4	5	6	7	8	9	10	11	12	13	14
Chili				✓				✓				✓		
Chocolate pie			✓			✓			✓			✓		

Solution: 1 day

4.

Order	1	2	3	4	5	6	7	8	9	10	11	12	13	14	15	16	17	18	19	20
Special		✓		✓		✓		✓		✓		✓		✓		✓		✓		✓
Dessert			✓			✓			✓			✓			✓			✓		
Soft drink				✓					✓			✓						✓		

Solution: 3 people

Pages 112 and 113

1. 13 yd.
2. 11 ft.
3. 3 ft.
4. 9 ft.
5. 8 ft.
6. 48 in.
7. 60 in. x 96 in.
8. 24 ft.
9. 4 yd.
10. 108 in.
11. 7 ft.
12. 96 in.
13. 6 ft.
14. 4 ft. x 6 ft.

Page 114

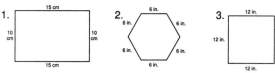
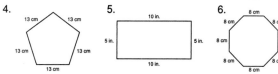
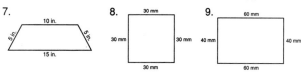
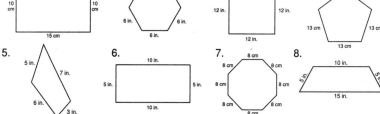
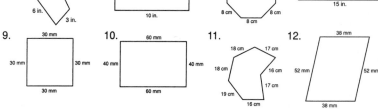

Page 115

Page 116

Page 117

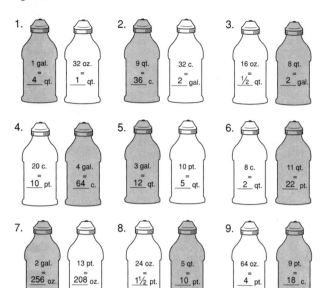

1. 1 gal. = **4** qt. | 32 oz. = **1** qt.
2. 9 qt. = **36** c. | 32 c. = **2** gal.
3. 16 oz. = **½** qt. | 8 qt. = **2** gal.
4. 20 c. = **10** pt. | 4 gal. = **64** c.
5. 3 gal. = **12** qt. | 10 pt. = **5** qt.
6. 8 c. = **2** qt. | 11 qt. = **22** pt.
7. 2 gal. = **256** oz. | 13 pt. = **208** oz.
8. 24 oz. = **1½** pt. | 5 qt. = **10** pt.
9. 64 oz. = **4** pt. | 9 pt. = **18** c.

Page 118
1. 3,500 pounds
2. 5 quarts
3. 6 hours
4. greater than
5. 2 half-ton loads; 301 pounds left over
6. 1:00 A.M. on Monday
7. T. Rucker
8. about 10 years

Page 119
1. 3,500 pounds
2. 72°F
3. 5 quarts
4. 5 hours 25 minutes
5. greater than
6. 2 half-ton loads; 301 pounds left over
7. 1:00 A.M. on Monday
8. 4 fluid ounces
9. T. Rucker
10. about 10 years

Page 120

Date	Beginning Time	Ending Time	Total Time Worked
1. Mon., Nov. 12	6:15 P.M.	8:30 P.M.	2 hrs. 15 mins.
2. Fri., Nov. 16	5:30 P.M.	10:20 P.M.	**4 hrs. 50 mins.**
3. Sat., Nov. 17	7:15 P.M.	11:50 P.M.	**4 hrs. 35 mins.**
4. Wed., Nov. 21	5:30 P.M.	9:20 P.M.	**3 hrs. 50 mins.**
5. Fri., Nov. 23	6:45 P.M.	10:20 P.M.	**3 hrs. 35 mins.**
6. Sat., Nov. 24	10:15 A.M.	4:00 P.M.	**5 hrs. 45 mins.**
7. Mon., Nov. 26	7:30 P.M.	9:45 P.M.	**2 hrs. 15 mins.**
8. Fri., Nov. 30	3:15 P.M.	10:40 P.M.	**7 hrs. 25 mins.**
9. Sat., Dec. 1	**10:20 A.M.**	2:35 P.M.	4 hrs. 15 mins.
10. Thurs., Dec. 6	5:50 P.M.	8:40 P.M.	**2 hrs. 50 mins.**
11. Fri., Dec. 7	**5:50 P.M.**	12:15 A.M.	6 hrs. 25 mins.
12. Sat., Dec. 8	11:45 A.M.	**5:15 P.M.**	5 hrs. 30 mins.

13. 3:10 P.M. (4:15 P.M. – 65 mins.)

Page 121

Date	Beginning Time	Ending Time	Total Time Worked
1. Mon., Nov. 12	6:15 P.M.	8:30 P.M.	2 hrs. 15 mins.
2. Fri., Nov. 16	5:30 P.M.	10:20 P.M.	**4 hrs. 50 mins.**
3. Sat., Nov. 17	7:15 P.M.	**11:50 P.M.**	4 hrs. 35 mins.
4. Wed., Nov. 21	**5:30 P.M.**	9:20 P.M.	3 hrs. 50 mins.
5. Fri., Nov. 23	6:45 P.M.	**10:20 P.M.**	3 hrs. 35 mins.
6. Sat., Nov. 24	10:15 A.M.	4:00 P.M.	**5 hrs. 45 mins.**
7. Mon., Nov. 26	7:30 P.M.	9:45 P.M.	**2 hrs. 15 mins.**
8. Fri., Nov. 30	3:15 P.M.	**10:40 P.M.**	7 hrs. 25 mins.
9. Sat., Dec. 1	**10:20 A.M.**	2:35 P.M.	4 hrs. 15 mins.
10. Thurs., Dec. 6	5:50 P.M.	8:40 P.M.	**2 hrs. 50 mins.**
11. Fri., Dec. 7	**5:50 P.M.**	12:15 A.M.	6 hrs. 25 mins.
12. Sat., Dec. 8	11:45 A.M.	**5:15 P.M.**	5 hrs. 30 mins.

13. 3:10 P.M. (4:15 P.M. – 65 mins.)
14. 8:45 A.M. (10:00 A.M. – 75 mins.)

Page 122

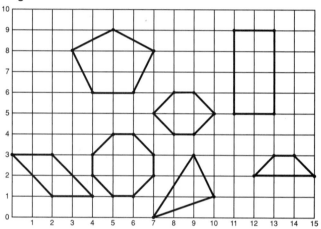

Page 123
1. parallelogram
2. octagon
3. triangle
4. trapezoid
5. hexagon
6. rectangle
7. pentagon

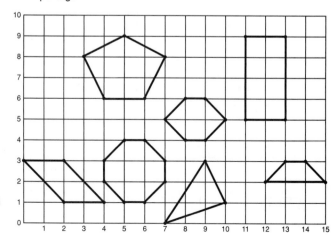

Page 124

1. line, red
2. both, blue
3. point, yellow
4. both, blue
5. neither, green
6. line, red
7. both, blue
8. line, red
9. both, blue

Page 125

1. line, red
2. both, blue
3. point, yellow
4. both, blue
5. neither, green
6. line, red
7. both, blue
8. line, red
9. point, yellow
10. both, blue
11. neither, green
12. point, yellow

Page 126

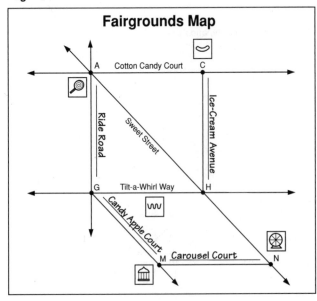

Page 127

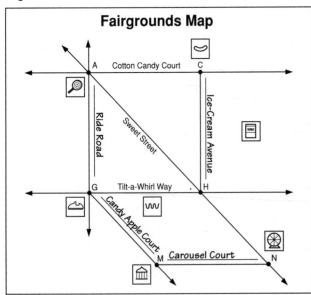

Page 128

1. acute
2. right
3. acute
4. acute
5. obtuse
6. right
7. obtuse
8. acute
9. obtuse
10. acute
11. obtuse
12. right

Page 129

1. acute
2. right
3. acute
4. obtuse
5. acute
6. obtuse
7. right
8. acute
9. obtuse
10. acute
11. obtuse
12. right
13. acute
14. obtuse
15. right
16. acute

Pages 130 and 131

1. Item: Square Pyramid
   Number of edges: 8
   Number of vertices: 5
   Number of faces: 5

2. Item: Cube
   Number of edges: 12
   Number of vertices: 8
   Number of faces: 6

3. Item: Triangular Pyramid
   Number of edges: 6
   Number of vertices: 4
   Number of faces: 4

4. Item: Rectangular Prism
   Number of edges: 12
   Number of vertices: 8
   Number of faces: 6

5. Item: Sphere
   Number of edges: 0
   Number of vertices: 0
   Number of faces: 0

6. Item: Triangular Prism
   Number of edges: 9
   Number of vertices: 6
   Number of faces: 5

Pages 132 and 133

Part 1
1. translation
2. reflection
3. rotation
4. reflection
5. rotation

Part 2
1. c
2. a
3. e
4. b
5. d

Page 134

1.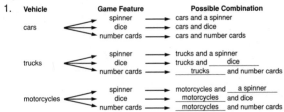

2. 9
3. 1 out of 9
4. 1 out of 9, or $\frac{1}{9}$

5.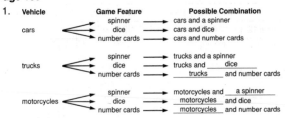

Page 135

1.

2. 9
3. 1 out of 9
4. 1 out of 9, or $\frac{1}{9}$

5.

Page 136

						Mean	Median	Mode	Range
Sparky X. Plode	$25	$27	$25	$31	$32	$28	$27	$25	$7
Bea Lastoff	$42	$65	$29	$47	$42	$45	$47	$42	$36
Iggie Nite	$38	$39	$38	$38	$32	$37	$38	$38	$7
Flash N. Boom	$14	$30	$26	$14	$76	$32	$26	$14	$62

A.
1. Bea Lastoff
2. Flash N. Boom, $76
3. Flash N. Boom and Bea Lastoff

B.
1. There are 20 numbers. The median is between the 10th and 11th numbers. 32
2. $38
3. $62

Page 137

								Mean	Median	Mode	Range
Sparky X. Plode	$25	$27	$26	$25	$31	$30	$25	$27	$26	$25	$6
Bea Lastoff	$42	$48	$65	$29	$47	$42	$49	$46	$47	$42	$36
Iggie Nite	$38	$39	$38	$40	$35	$32	$37	$37	$38	$38	$8
Flash N. Boom	$14	$29	$21	$58	$26	$14	$76	$34	$26	$14	$62

A.
1. Bea Lastoff
2. Flash N. Boom, $76
3. Flash N. Boom and Bea Lastoff
4. About $38; Iggie's mean, or average, amount of money collected is $37.

Stem	Leaves
1	4 4
2	1 5 5 5 6 6 7 9 9
3	0 1 2 5 7 8 8 9
4	0 2 2 7 8 9
5	8
6	5
7	6

B.
1. $36
2. There are 28 numbers. The median is between the 14th and 15th numbers. (32 + 35) ÷ 2 = 33.5 or 34
3. $25
4. $62

Page 138
Part 1

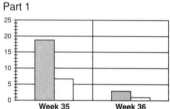

Part 2
1. week 34; 21 cans
2. week 36; 1 bottle
3. cans
4. The graph is easier to read because the numbers are represented as pictures. It's easier to see it at a glance.

Page 139
Part 1

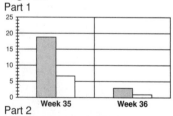

Part 2
1. week 34; 21 cans
2. week 36; 1 bottle
3. cans
4. The graph is easier to read because the numbers are represented as pictures. It's easier to see it at a glance.
5. The garbage cans were probably installed between weeks 35 and 36 because the number of items found on the ground dropped significantly between those weeks.

Page 140
1. 25
2. 10
3. 20
4. January, February, and April

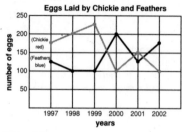

Page 141
1. 25
2. 10
3. 20
4. January, February, and April

Students' graphs may vary slightly. One possible graph is shown.

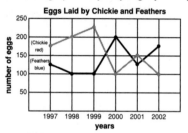

Pages 142 and 143
1. Rule D; 34, 41
2. Rule H; 324, 972
3. Rule A; 120, 40
4. Rule E; 50, 35
5. Rule B; 121, 176
6. Rule J; 18, 21
7. Rule C; 55, 64
8. Rule G; 17, 23
9. Rule F; 22, …, 59
10. Rule I; 48, …, 6

Page 144
Numbers are listed from top to bottom.
1. 15, 21, 27, 36
2. 7, 12, 16, 23
3. 4, 25, 29, 21
4. 2, 36, 9, 66
5. 8, 11, 18, 24
6. 3, 45, 7, 90

Page 145
Numbers are listed from top to bottom.
1. 15, 21, 27, 36
2. 7, 12, 16, 23
3. 4, 25, 29, 21
4. 2, 36, 9, 66
5. 8, 11, 18, 24
6. 3, 45, 7, 90
7. 15, 5, 11, 1
8. 2, 4, 56, 96

In the…DOGHOUSE!

Page 146
Numbers are listed from top to bottom.
1. 11, 17
2. 32, 8
3. 45, 6, 24
4. 5, 29, 23
5. 2, 10, 36
6. 6, 12

Page 147
Numbers are listed from top to bottom.
2. 32, 8; rule: x 8
3. 45, 6, 24; rule: ÷ 3
4. 5, 29, 23; rule: − 9
5. 2, 10, 36; rule: x 12
6. 6, 12; rule: x 2, + 1
7. 50, 9; rule: ÷ 5, + 4
8. 19, 12; rule: − 3, ÷ 2
9. 12, 65, 4; rule: x 4, + 5